Welcome

I t's time to enjoy the loveliest and most exciting season of the year with *Country Woman Christmas 2004!*

We've filled this annual keepsake edition cover to cover with the sights, sounds, scents and spirit of the holidays.

Inside, you'll find all the makings for a hearth-warming family celebration—from jolly decorating tips and tantalizing family-favorite recipes to merry do-it-yourself crafts, gifts and pretty party ideas.

We've also tucked in some nostalgic stories and true-life memories, traditional Christmas carols, whimsical poems and uplifting profiles of country women with creative ideas for bringing the holidays home.

So light the candles, crank up the carols and put those finishing touches on your tree. Then gather friends and family together to enjoy all the warmth and love of a country Christmas—blessed with our wishes for hope and goodwill in the year to come.

Table of Contents

…and Much More!

30

84

100

Executive Editor
Kathy Pohl

Editor
Kathleen Anderson

Food Editor
Janaan Cunningham

Art Director
Emma Acevedo

Associate Editor
Mary C. Hanson

Associate Food Editor
Diane Werner

Senior Home Economist
Karen Wright

Senior Recipe Editor
Sue A. Jurack

Recipe Editor
Janet Briggs

Craft Editor
Jane Craig

Art Associate
Tom Hunt

Proofreader
Kris Krueger

Editorial Assistant
Joanne Wied

Test Kitchen Assistant
Rita Krajcir

Food Stylists
Joylyn Trickel, Kristin Koepnick

Studio Photographers
Rob Hagen, Dan Roberts

Food Photography Artists
Stephanie Marchese
Julie Ferron

Photo Studio Manager
Anne Schimmel

Graphic Art Associates
Ellen Lloyd, Catherine Fletcher

Chairman and Founder
Roy Reiman

President
Russell Denson

©2004 Reiman Media Group, Inc.
5400 S. 60th Street
Greendale WI 53129

International Standard Book Number:
0-89821-408-4
International Standard Serial Number:
1093-6750

All rights reserved. Printed in U.S.A.

PICTURED ON OUR COVER. Shown clockwise from upper left: Happy Holiday Horse Trims (p. 97), Frosted Fantasy Tree Cookies (p. 50), Easy Chocolate Truffles (p. 28), Jolly Santa Treat Cup (p. 86) and Homemade Gumdrops in merry Christmas colors (p. 27).

Memories Trim Her Holiday Home And Brighten Christmas Season!

HOME FOR THE HOLIDAYS means a cozy cabin strung with twinkly lights, evergreen garlands and plenty of memories, according to Wendy Gibbons of New Lenox, Illinois.

"Memories are what's important at Christmas," she says with a smile. "I never throw out any decorations made by someone in the family. You can *always* find a place for something that holds a memory."

From the merry old sled and antique skis that deck her front entry to the nostalgic Christmas collectibles she has tucked in every corner, her spacious log home wraps family, friends and neighborhood carolers in a warm Yuletide welcome.

"From your first step inside, our kitchen, eating area and great room are all within view, so you get a special feeling of togetherness," says Wendy, who literally built that feeling into the house herself.

"I love entertaining over the holidays and didn't want to be isolated out in the kitchen," she explains. "So 16 years ago when we decided to build a new home, I sketched out the kind of open concept I wanted, and the architect followed my design."

Out the window, century-old oaks, wildlife and pine trees planted by her father fill a yard that was once pastureland for her grandparents' cattle.

One of those 12-foot pines, now glittering with ornaments and lights beside the brick fireplace in her great room, throws a rich glow on log walls and butternut wood floors. Beneath its branches, old toys—many of them favorites of her four grown children—circle the base with happy memories.

"One year I'll use colored lights, the next year I'll have only white ones —mini, regular, frosted antique-looking ones and bubble lights all together," she says.

"I love mixing old with new…vintage ornaments from my grandmother with new craft items. It cuts costs and adds interest. Plus, if the kids wanted to rearrange trims, I never wanted them to feel that the decorations were too special to handle."

The More, the Merrier

Holiday decorating should be fun, Wendy believes. "I don't try to copy something I see in a store but prefer to use things from everywhere and everybody," she relates.

Colorful ornaments handmade by her children, nieces and nephews as they were growing up are tucked all

STOCKINGS HUNG BY THE CHIMNEY WITH CARE, a glowing fire, the warm scent of cinnamon and oranges simmering on the stove greet family, friends and visitors to Wendy Gibbons' Illinois home. "I love to entertain at Christmas. I don't like froufrou, but I grew up on a farm and just love old things—the history in them," Wendy says, adding that it takes her about 2 weeks to tuck a lifetime of Yuletide treasures and collectibles into every corner. Below, the whole family gathers 'round a quilt-covered table to celebrate their holiday tradition of eating hot fudge sundaes after watching the Christmas classic *It's a Wonderful Life* together.

Photos: George Ploetner Photography

through the house. "I bring them out every year and put them in a different place," she notes. "Every year those grown-up kids search for their masterpieces when they come over!"

In one corner, an antique baker's rack holds a Nativity set hand-carved in Israel and now housed in one of the many antique toy barns Wendy has collected over the years.

An old pine hutch on another wall holds more seasonal treasures. "That was a great flea-market find," she recalls. "It's just perfect for all my antique bowls and couldn't work out nicer for displaying my holiday collections."

Snowmen, feather trees and Santa figures in all sizes and shapes can be seen in every room. Made of ceramic, fabric, papier-mache, wood, cross-stitch, glass and more, her St. Nicks are grouped in an old berry strainer in one room and piled on baskets in another. They straddle the kitchen windowsills, too, along with old-fashioned wooden blocks spelling out "Merry Christmas".

"Grouping things together—even poinsettias—always makes more of a statement," Wendy says. "I like doing things at different levels, layering or stacking items to add a sense of dimension."

A bank of candles in antique bobbins of various heights creates a warm relaxing atmosphere in front of her fireplace. "It gives the same effect as a roaring fire, but it's much less drying on the nearby tree and mantel trims," she explains.

In the dining area, a small silver tree tops a quilt-covered table brightened by flickering tea lights set in old glass casters from her grandmother's bed. An overhead chandelier shines with vintage glass beads and fragrant greenery.

Nearby, more pine garlands light up the banister behind another tree trimmed in cheery folk-art ornaments. "Cleaning up all the dry needles every year is a real chore," Wendy admits, "but that pine aroma is a Christmas favorite."

So are the traditional hot fudge sundaes she serves up every year when her entire clan gathers to watch *It's a Wonderful Life* together. Family gatherings, candlelight and carols, precious memories nestled in every corner…it's another keepsake Christmas at Wendy's house!

A PAINTED SLED and old pair of skis under evergreen boughs aglow with lights hint at the nostalgia of merry Christmases past that fill each nook and cranny of Wendy's log cabin. Above, a tree shimmers with antique trims and once-cherished toys of four children now grown.

Christmastime

Candles in the windows
Lights upon the tree,
Holly wreath hangs on the door—
A pretty sight to see.

Doorways framed in evergreen,
Fragrant fir and pine,
A creche upon the mantel,
Children's eyes a-shine.

Whispered conversations,
Happy secrets by the score,
Brightly bundled packages
'Neath tree and on the floor.

Cherub voices singing
Christmas carols sweet,
Candy, nuts and popcorn balls,
All things good to eat.

Yule logs burning brightly,
A bit of mistletoe;
Lights upon a tree outside
Drop rainbows on the snow.

Laughter, love and kindness;
Each one plays a part
In spreading Christmas through the house
As well as to the heart.

—*Lucille King*
Mifflinburg, Pennsylvania

Glad Tidings...

Christmas Wishes

A MERRY CHRISTMAS

GLORIA

A merry Christmas

ACROSS THE MILES and through the years, Christmas cards have become a cherished holiday tradition. Beginning in the mid-1800s, lithographers often used as many as 26 glowing colors in the penny-postcards now treasured as collectibles. Here are some examples from Bonnie Ziolecki of Menomonee Falls, Wisconsin.

Jingle Bell Brunch

BREAKFAST BELL-RINGERS shown clockwise from top right: Bacon Broccoli Quiche (p. 14), Honey-Lime Fruit Dip (p. 15), Peaches 'n' Cream French Toast (p. 14), Glazed Poppy Seed Doughnuts (p. 14) and Hot Cran-Apple Cider (p. 14).

Open everyone's eyes on Christmas morning with a mouth-watering buffet of festive foods sure to warm hearts and spark a merry rise-and-shine mood.

BACON BROCCOLI QUICHE
Karren Fairbanks, Salt Lake City, Utah
(Pictured on page 13)

Even folks who claim not to like quiche rave about this one! I developed the recipe by combining the best of five others that I'd tried. Now it's a hearty family favorite that always gets star billing at my traditional Christmas morning brunch.

      2 tablespoons all-purpose flour
  1/2 cup mayonnaise*
      1 tablespoon dried minced onion
      1 tablespoon butter, melted
      1 teaspoon salt
      3 eggs
1-1/2 cups milk
      1 package (10 ounces) frozen chopped broccoli,
         thawed and patted dry
    12 bacon strips, cooked and crumbled
      8 medium fresh mushrooms, chopped
      2 cups (8 ounces) shredded Monterey Jack cheese
      1 sheet refrigerated pie pastry

In a large bowl, combine the first five ingredients. Whisk in eggs, one at a time. Stir in the milk, broccoli, bacon, mushrooms and cheese. Line a 9-in. deep-dish pie plate with pastry. Trim pastry to 1/2 in. beyond edge of plate; flute edges. Pour broccoli mixture into crust. Bake at 350° for 55-60 minutes or until a knife inserted near the center comes out clean. Let stand for 10-15 minutes before cutting. **Yield:** 6-8 servings.
   *Editor's Note: Reduced-fat or fat-free mayonnaise is not recommended for this recipe.

PEACHES 'N' CREAM FRENCH TOAST
Tiffany Mitchell, Susanville, California
(Pictured on page 12)

Looking for a way to make French toast into something extra special? This scrumptious breakfast dish is topped with peach butter and bursting with flavor. Whip it up the night before and grill in minutes on a busy Christmas morning.

      3 eggs
      3 tablespoons plus 1/3 cup peach preserves,
         divided
  3/4 cup half-and-half cream
      8 slices French bread (1/2 inch thick)
      6 tablespoons butter (no substitutes), softened,
         divided
Confectioners' sugar
Sliced almonds, toasted
      2 medium ripe peaches, sliced

In a small bowl, beat eggs and 3 tablespoons preserves. Add cream; mix well. Arrange bread in a single layer in a 13-in. x 9-in. x 2-in. dish. Pour egg mixture over bread; cover and refrigerate overnight.
   For peach butter, beat 4 tablespoons butter and re-maining preserves in a small mixing bowl until fluffy; set aside. Cook bread slices in remaining butter on a hot grid-dle until golden brown on each side. Sprinkle with confec-tioners' sugar and almonds. Serve with peach butter and sliced peaches. **Yield:** 4 servings.

HOT CRAN-APPLE CIDER
Alice Tatro, Geneva, Nebraska
(Pictured on page 12)

This sparkly refreshing fruit drink is part of every holiday oc-casion I host. A tangy twist on plain apple cider, it fills the house with warm Christmas aromas as it simmers.

  3/4 teaspoon whole cloves
      1 medium navel orange
      1 medium lemon
      1 quart apple cider *or* juice
      3 cups cranberry juice
      2 tablespoons brown sugar
      2 cinnamon sticks (3 inches)

Insert cloves into orange. Cut orange and lemon into slices. In a large saucepan, combine the remaining ingredients; add orange and lemon slices. Bring to a boil. Reduce heat; simmer, uncovered, for 30 minutes. Remove cinnamon sticks and fruit slices with slotted spoon if desired before serving. Ladle into mugs. **Yield:** 6-8 servings.

GLAZED POPPY SEED DOUGHNUTS
Pat Hawryliw, Saskatoon, Saskatchewan
(Pictured on page 12)

Light as a feather, these pretty glazed doughnuts are my husband's all-time favorites. They're something to celebrate any time of year at all!

      1 tablespoon active dry yeast
      1 teaspoon plus 1/2 cup sugar, *divided*
      1 cup warm water (110° to 115°)
  2/3 cup warm milk (110° to 115°)
  1/3 cup poppy seeds
  1/2 cup shortening
      1 cup warm mashed potatoes (prepared without
         milk and butter)
      3 eggs
      7 to 8 cups all-purpose flour
      1 teaspoon salt
      1 teaspoon ground cinnamon
Vegetable oil for deep-fat frying
GLAZE:
  1/2 cup sugar
  1/4 cup milk
  1/4 cup butter, cubed
  1/2 cup confectioners' sugar
  1/4 teaspoon salt
  1/4 teaspoon vanilla extract

In a large mixing bowl, dissolve yeast and 1 teaspoon sugar in warm water. In another bowl, combine milk and poppy seeds. Let each bowl stand for 5 minutes.

Add shortening and remaining sugar to yeast mixture; mix well. Add potatoes and eggs; beat well. Add the poppy seed mixture, 3 cups flour, salt and cinnamon; beat until smooth. Stir in enough remaining flour to form a soft dough. Turn onto a floured surface; knead until smooth and elastic, about 6-8 minutes. Place in a greased bowl, turning once to grease top. Cover and let rise in a warm place until doubled, about 1 hour.

Punch dough down. Turn onto a lightly floured surface; divide into fourths. Roll out each portion to 1/2-in. thickness. Cut with a floured 2-1/2-in. doughnut cutter. Place on greased baking sheets. Cover and let rise for 30 minutes.

In an electric skillet or deep-fat fryer, heat oil to 375°. Fry doughnuts, a few at a time, for 1-1/2 minutes on each side or until golden brown. Drain on paper towels.

In a saucepan, bring sugar, milk and butter to a boil. Cook and stir for 1 minute. Remove from the heat; cool completely. Stir in confectioners' sugar, salt and vanilla until smooth. Drizzle over doughnuts. **Yield:** 3-1/2 dozen.

HONEY-LIME FRUIT DIP
Karen McBride, Indianapolis, Indiana
(Pictured on page 13)

For more than 20 years, this citrusy dip has been as welcome as sunshine at our holiday breakfast table. Try serving it with fresh melon, pineapple, green apples, strawberries, kiwis and bananas.

    1 egg, beaten
1/2 cup honey
1/4 cup lime juice
Dash salt
Dash ground mace
    1 cup (8 ounces) sour cream
Assorted fresh fruit

In a small saucepan, combine the egg, honey and lime juice. Cook and stir over medium heat until mixture reaches 160° and is thickened. Remove from the heat; stir in salt and mace. Cool to room temperature. Stir in the sour cream. Cover and refrigerate for 1 hour or until chilled. Serve with fruit. **Yield:** 2 cups.

BREAKFAST BRAID
Carol Happley, Jordan, Minnesota
(Pictured at right)

I created this recipe years ago and was thrilled when it won first prize in a newspaper cooking contest. Stuffed with ham, cheese and olives, it's hearty enough to satisfy Santa himself.

3-3/4 to 4-1/4 cups all-purpose flour
  2/3 cup shredded cheddar cheese
  1/3 cup grated Romano cheese
    1 envelope onion soup mix
    2 tablespoons sugar
    2 packages (1/4 ounce *each*) active dry yeast

    1 teaspoon salt
  3/4 cup milk
  1/4 cup water
    3 tablespoons butter, softened
    3 eggs
FILLING:
1-1/2 cups (6 ounces) shredded cheddar cheese
1-1/2 cups diced fully cooked ham
  1/3 cup shredded mozzarella cheese
  1/3 cup diced green pepper
  1/3 cup diced onion
    1 jar (2 ounces) chopped pimientos, drained
    3 tablespoons chopped stuffed olives
    3 tablespoons butter, melted, *divided*
Additional Romano cheese

In a large mixing bowl, combine 2 cups flour, cheeses, soup mix, sugar, yeast and salt; mix well. In a saucepan, heat milk, water and butter to 120°-130°. Add to dry ingredients; beat until moistened. Add eggs; beat on medium speed for 2 minutes. Stir in enough remaining flour to form a soft dough. Turn onto a floured surface; knead until smooth and elastic, about 8-10 minutes. Place in a greased bowl, turning once to grease top. Cover and let rise in a warm place until doubled, about 1 hour.

For filling, in a bowl, combine the cheddar cheese, ham, mozzarella cheese, green pepper, onion, pimientos and olives; refrigerate until ready to use. Punch dough down. Turn onto a lightly floured surface; divide in half. Roll out each portion into a 12-in. x 10-in. rectangle. Place on greased baking sheets.

Spread filling down the center of each rectangle. Drizzle each with 2 teaspoons butter. On each long side, cut 3/4-in.-wide strips on a diagonal, about 2-1/2 in. into center. Starting at one end, fold alternating strips at an angle across filling. Pinch ends to seal. Cover and let rise in a warm place until doubled, about 45 minutes.

Bake at 350° for 20-25 minutes or until browned and cheese is melted. Remove from pans to wire racks. Brush with remaining butter and sprinkle with additional Romano cheese. Serve warm. Refrigerate leftovers. **Yield:** 2 loaves.

APPLE DUTCH BABY
Teeny McCloy, Red Deer, Alberta

This dish is a longtime family favorite for Christmas morning. It's light and airy, filled with eggs and juicy apples and delicious with bacon on the side.

    1/4 cup butter
       3 to 4 medium tart apples, peeled and sliced
    1/4 cup packed brown sugar
       1 teaspoon ground cinnamon
       6 eggs, *separated*
    2/3 cup all-purpose flour
    1/3 cup milk
       1 teaspoon baking powder
    1/2 teaspoon salt
    1/4 cup sugar

Place butter in a 13-in. x 9-in. x 2-in. baking dish. Heat at 400° for 5-8 minutes or until melted. Add apples, brown sugar and cinnamon; mix well. Bake 15-18 minutes longer or until apples are tender.

Meanwhile, in a bowl, whisk the egg yolks, flour, milk, baking powder and salt. In a mixing bowl, beat the egg whites on medium speed until soft peaks form. Gradually add sugar, 1 tablespoon at a time, beating on high until stiff peaks form. Fold into egg yolk mixture. Spread over apples. Bake at 400° for 12-15 minutes or until set and golden. **Yield:** 8 servings.

ITALIAN SPINACH SAUSAGE PIE
Erla Johnson, Peoria, Illinois

Christmas at our house is a celebration of tradition. No matter how many guests we might have, our morning brunch has not varied for years. It's always this festive sausage pie served with stollen and fruit salad.

       1 pound bulk Italian sausage
       6 eggs
       2 packages (10 ounces *each*) frozen chopped
          spinach, thawed and squeezed dry
       4 cups (16 ounces) shredded mozzarella cheese
    3/4 cup ricotta cheese
    1/2 teaspoon salt
    1/8 teaspoon garlic powder
    1/8 teaspoon pepper
Pastry for a double-crust pie (10 inches)
       1 tablespoon water

In a skillet, cook sausage over medium heat until no longer pink; drain. Separate one egg and set the yolk aside. In a mixing bowl, beat the egg white and remaining eggs. Add the spinach, mozzarella cheese, ricotta cheese, salt, garlic powder, pepper and sausage; mix well.

Line a 10-in. pie plate with bottom pastry. Add filling. Roll out remaining pastry to fit top of pie; place over filling. Trim, seal and flute edges. Cut slits in pastry. If desired, cut out holly leaf and berry shapes from pastry scraps; place on top crust. Beat water and remaining egg yolk; brush over top.

Bake at 375° for 50-60 minutes or until crust is golden brown and filling is bubbly. Let stand for 10 minutes before cutting. **Yield:** 8 servings.

CRANBROSIA GELATIN MOLD
Gladys McCollum Abee, McKee, Kentucky
(Pictured above)

Guests "ooh" and "aah" when I bring out this frosty fruit-filled ring. Garnished with mint, sugared cranberries and mandarin oranges, it's one brunch showstopper that's pretty enough to serve as dessert!

       2 cups fresh *or* frozen cranberries, coarsely ground
       1 cup sugar
       1 can (11 ounces) mandarin oranges
       1 can (8 ounces) sliced pineapple
       2 envelopes unflavored gelatin
       1 cup (8 ounces) sour cream
       1 cup heavy whipping cream
       2 tablespoons confectioners' sugar

In a bowl, combine cranberries and sugar. Let stand for 30 minutes or until sugar is dissolved, stirring occasionally. Drain juice from oranges and pineapple, reserving 3/4 cup juice. Cut pineapple into small pieces. Set fruit aside.

In a small saucepan, sprinkle gelatin over reserved juice; let stand for 1 minute. Cook and stir over low heat until gelatin is dissolved, about 2 minutes. Add to cranberry mixture; stir in the oranges and pineapple. Fold in sour cream.

In a small mixing bowl, beat cream until it begins to thicken. Add confectioners' sugar; beat until soft peaks form. Fold into fruit mixture. Pour into a 6-cup ring mold or 12 individual molds lightly coated with nonstick cooking spray. Refrigerate until set. Unmold before serving. **Yield:** 10-12 servings.

SAUSAGE CHEESE BRUNCH SQUARES
Pat Stevens, Granbury, Texas

Here's a cheesy sausage dish that always gives my breakfast crowd a stick-to-the-ribs jump start on Christmas morning.

 1 cup biscuit/baking mix
 1/3 cup milk
 4 tablespoons mayonnaise*, *divided*
 1 pound bulk pork sausage
 1 cup chopped onion
 1 egg
 2 cans (4 ounces *each*) chopped green chilies
 2 cups (8 ounces) shredded cheddar cheese

In a bowl, combine the biscuit mix, milk and 2 tablespoons mayonnaise. Spread into a greased 11-in. x 7-in. x 2-in. baking dish.

In a large skillet, cook the sausage and onion over medium heat until meat is no longer pink; drain. Spoon over biscuit mixture.

In a bowl, combine the egg, chilies and remaining mayonnaise; spread over sausage mixture. Sprinkle with cheese. Bake, uncovered, at 350° for 30-35 minutes or until golden brown. **Yield:** 6-8 servings.

*Editor's Note: Reduced-fat or fat-free mayonnaise is not recommended for this recipe.

BRUNCH POCKETS
Jean Kimm, Coeur d'Alene, Idaho

These hefty handfuls promise everyone a good hot breakfast with little fuss. Kids especially love the toasty grab-and-go pockets stuffed with pineapple, ham, turkey and cheese. And what a great way to use up leftovers!

 1 package (15 ounces) refrigerated pie crust
 2 pineapple slices, cut in half
 4 thin slices deli ham
 4 thin slices deli turkey
 4 slices Swiss cheese
 1 egg, beaten

Cut each pastry sheet into four wedges. Pat pineapple slices dry with paper towels. Top four pastry wedges with one slice each of ham, turkey, cheese and pineapple, folding meat and cheese to fit if necessary. Top each with a pastry wedge; seal and crimp edges with a fork. Cut slits in pastry.

Place on an ungreased baking sheet. Brush lightly with egg. Bake at 350° for 25-30 minutes or until golden brown. Serve warm. **Yield:** 4 servings.

PEPPERED SHRIMP AND EGGS
Francis Connor, Canton, Ohio

Talk about your gourmet eggs…this breakfast dish is so easy to make but just shouts "company's here"! The savory recipe came from a friend, and we save it for holidays and special guests throughout the year.

 3 bacon strips, diced
 3/4 cup chopped green pepper

 1/2 cup chopped onion
 6 eggs
 1/4 cup half-and-half cream
 1/2 teaspoon salt
 1/4 teaspoon cayenne pepper
 1/2 pound cooked large shrimp, peeled, deveined and halved

In a large skillet, cook bacon over medium heat until crisp. Remove with a slotted spoon to paper towels; drain, reserving 2 tablespoons drippings.

In the drippings, saute green pepper and onion until tender. In a bowl, whisk the eggs, cream, salt and cayenne; add to the vegetable mixture. Add shrimp and bacon. Cook and stir until the eggs are completely set. **Yield:** 6 servings.

OVERNIGHT MUSHROOM EGG CASSEROLE
Jennifer Green, Chattanooga, Tennessee

Want to be sure your family's eggs are all ready at the same time on Christmas morning? Try this merry make-ahead breakfast casserole. I sometimes make it heartier by adding some dried beef with the bacon.

 5 tablespoons butter, *divided*
 1/3 cup all-purpose flour
 1-1/2 cups milk
 1 jar (4-1/2 ounces) sliced mushrooms, drained
 10 eggs
 2/3 cup half-and-half cream
 1/4 teaspoon salt
 1/8 teaspoon pepper
 10 bacon strips, cooked and crumbled

In a saucepan, melt 3 tablespoons butter. Stir in flour until smooth; gradually add milk. Bring to a boil; cook and stir for 2 minutes or until thickened. Stir in the mushrooms; set aside.

In a bowl, whisk the eggs, cream, salt and pepper. In a skillet, heat the remaining butter until hot. Add egg mixture; cook and stir over medium heat until eggs are completely set. Transfer to a greased 11-in. x 7-in. x 2-in. baking dish; top with mushroom mixture. Sprinkle with bacon. Cover and refrigerate overnight.

Remove from the refrigerator 30 minutes before baking. Bake, uncovered, at 325° for 32-36 minutes or until heated through. **Yield:** 12 servings.

IN ALL THE HUSTLE and bustle of planning your holiday brunch, it's easy to overlook the fact that guests will need something to drink along with their food. Here are some tips to remember:

● In addition to milk and coffee, a sparkling fruit or cider punch with a pretty ice ring makes a merry addition to any table. Remember that a 1-gallon bowl of punch will yield about 24 servings.

● Coffee begins to lose its flavor within an hour after it's made and gets a bitter taste if heated too long. Keep it hot in a thermos or carafe and brew more as needed.

Festive Breads

Kindle warm memories of Christmases past with the down-home aroma of fresh-baked breads, muffins and rolls all through the house.

CURRANT TEA BREAD
Ruth Stenson, Santa Ana, California
(Pictured on page 18)

This rich and flavorful bread is a favorite old-time recipe. Because it keeps well and goes great with coffee or tea, I like to have an extra loaf on hand for gifts or for friends who come to call over the holidays.

    1/4 cup butter, softened
      1 cup sugar
      2 eggs
    1/2 cup milk
1-1/2 teaspoons grated lemon peel
      2 cups all-purpose flour
    1/2 teaspoon baking powder
      1 cup dried currants

In a large mixing bowl, cream butter and sugar. Add the eggs, one at a time, beating well after each addition. Beat in the milk and lemon peel. Combine flour and baking powder; gradually add to the creamed mixture and mix well. Stir in the currants.

   Transfer to a greased 9-in. x 5-in. x 3-in. loaf pan. Bake at 350° for 55-60 minutes or until a toothpick inserted near the center comes out clean. Cool for 10 minutes before removing from pan to a wire rack. **Yield:** 1 loaf.

CRANBERRY CHRISTMAS CANES
Rita Fenley, Chesapeake, Virginia
(Pictured on page 18)

A festive shape, zesty cranberry filling and Christmas colors make these sweet rolls a real holiday hit with my crew. Sometimes I change the glaze, omitting the vanilla and using orange juice instead of milk for a tangier taste.

      4 cups all-purpose flour
    1/4 cup sugar
      1 teaspoon salt
      1 teaspoon grated lemon peel
      1 cup cold butter
      1 package (1/4 ounce) active dry yeast
    1/4 cup warm water (110° to 115°)
      1 cup warm milk (110° to 115°)
      2 eggs, beaten
FILLING:
1-1/2 cups finely chopped fresh *or* frozen cranberries
    1/2 cup sugar
    1/2 cup raisins
    1/3 cup chopped pecans
    1/3 cup honey
1-1/2 teaspoons grated orange peel

HOMEMADE HOLIDAY BREADS to share with your loved ones include delicious Cranberry Christmas Canes, quick and comforting Currant Tea Bread and rich French Chocolate Coffee Cake (p. 18, clockwise from lower right).

GLAZE:
1-1/2 cups confectioners' sugar
      2 tablespoons milk
    1/2 teaspoon vanilla extract

In a large bowl, combine the flour, sugar, salt and lemon peel; cut in butter until crumbly. In a small bowl, dissolve yeast in warm water. Add milk and eggs. Stir into flour mixture until blended. Cover and refrigerate overnight.

   In a saucepan, combine the filling ingredients. Bring to a boil over medium heat, stirring constantly. Cook and stir 5 minutes longer; cool.

   Punch dough down. Turn onto a lightly floured surface; divide in half. Roll one portion into an 18-in. x 15-in. rectangle. Spread filling to within 1/2 in. of edges. Fold one short side to center over filling; repeat with other side, making a 15-in. x 6-in. rectangle. Pinch seam to seal. Cut into 15 slices. Twist each slice and form a cane shape. Place 2 in. apart on greased baking sheets. Repeat with remaining dough and filling. Cover and let rise in a warm place until doubled, about 45 minutes.

   Bake at 400° for 12-14 minutes or until golden brown. Remove from pans to wire racks. Combine glaze ingredients; spread over rolls. **Yield:** 2-1/2 dozen.

FRENCH CHOCOLATE COFFEE CAKE
Julie Porter, Fishers, Indiana
(Pictured on page 18)

My mom always made this coffee cake as a special treat for us on Christmas morning. And my family loves the rich fudgy filling just as much as we did back then.

      1 package (1/4 ounce) active dry yeast
    2/3 cup warm water (110° to 115°)
    1/2 cup butter, softened
    3/4 cup sugar
      4 egg yolks
    1/3 cup evaporated milk
    1/2 teaspoon salt
3-3/4 to 4-1/4 cups all-purpose flour
FILLING:
    3/4 cup semisweet chocolate chips
    1/3 cup evaporated milk
      2 tablespoons sugar
    1/2 teaspoon ground cinnamon
TOPPING:
    1/4 cup all-purpose flour
    1/4 cup sugar
      1 teaspoon ground cinnamon
    1/4 cup cold butter
    1/4 cup semisweet chocolate chips
    1/4 cup chopped walnuts
Confectioners' sugar, optional

In a large mixing bowl, dissolve yeast in warm water. Add the butter, sugar, egg yolks, milk and salt; mix well. Add 2 cups flour; beat until smooth. Stir in enough remaining flour to form a soft dough. Turn onto a floured surface;

knead until smooth and elastic, about 6-8 minutes. Place in a greased bowl, turning once to grease top. Cover and let rise in a warm place until doubled, about 1 hour.

For filling, combine the chocolate chips, milk and sugar in a saucepan; cook and stir over low heat until smooth. Stir in cinnamon; set aside. For topping, combine the flour, sugar and cinnamon in a bowl; cut in butter until crumbly. Stir in chocolate chips and nuts. Set aside.

Punch dough down. Turn onto a lightly floured surface; roll into an 18-in. x 10-in. rectangle. Spread with filling. Roll up jelly-roll style, starting with a long side; pinch seam to seal. Place in a well-greased 10-in. fluted tube pan, with seam facing inside of pan. Sprinkle with topping. Cover and let rise in a warm place until doubled, about 30 minutes.

Bake at 350° for 45-50 minutes or until golden brown. Let stand for 10 minutes before inverting onto a wire rack to cool. Sprinkle with confectioners' sugar if desired. **Yield:** 12-16 servings.

BISHOP'S BREAD
Nikki Schoch, Rota, Spain

Packed with cherries, chocolate and nuts, this delectable quick bread has become a Christmas morning family tradition.

  2/3 cup butter, softened
  3/4 cup sugar
    2 eggs
    1 teaspoon vanilla extract
2-1/2 cups all-purpose flour
    3 teaspoons baking powder
  1/2 teaspoon salt
    1 cup milk
  1/3 cup semisweet chocolate chips
  1/3 cup raisins
  1/3 cup chopped pecans
  1/3 cup halved red and green candied cherries
GLAZE:
    1 cup confectioners' sugar
    2 tablespoons milk

In a large mixing bowl, cream butter and sugar. Add the eggs, one at a time, beating well after each addition. Beat in vanilla. Combine the flour, baking powder and salt; add to creamed mixture alternately with milk. Fold in the chocolate chips, raisins, pecans and candied cherries.

Transfer to a greased 9-in. x 5-in. x 3-in. loaf pan. Bake at 350° for 65-75 minutes or until a toothpick inserted near the center comes out clean. Cool for 10 minutes before removing from pan to a wire rack. Combine glaze ingredients; drizzle over warm bread. **Yield:** 1 loaf.

PEPPER JACK BATTER BREAD
Becky Asher, Salem, Oregon

This flavorful loaf is flecked with green chilies and hearty enough to turn a steaming bowl of soup into a meal.

    1 package (1/4 ounce) active dry yeast
  1/4 cup warm water (110° to 115°)
  1/2 cup warm milk (110° to 115°)
  1/3 cup butter, melted
    1 teaspoon salt
    2 eggs
2-1/4 to 2-3/4 cups all-purpose flour
  1/2 cup plus 2 tablespoons cornmeal, *divided*
    1 can (4 ounces) chopped green chilies, drained
    4 ounces pepper Jack cheese, shredded

In a large mixing bowl, dissolve yeast in warm water. Add the milk, butter, salt, eggs and 1 cup flour. Beat on low speed for 30 seconds. Beat on medium for 2 minutes. Stir in 1/2 cup cornmeal and remaining flour. Stir in chilies and cheese. Do not knead. Cover and let rise in a warm place until doubled, about 45 minutes.

Stir dough down. Sprinkle 1 tablespoon cornmeal into a greased 9-in. x 5-in. x 3-in. loaf pan. Spoon batter into pan. Sprinkle with remaining cornmeal. Cover and let rise in a warm place until doubled, about 30 minutes.

Bake at 375° for 45-50 minutes or until bread sounds hollow when tapped. Cool for 10 minutes before removing from pan to a wire rack. Store in the refrigerator. **Yield:** 1 loaf.

CHERRY COFFEE RING
Yolande Nolte, Clarksville, Tennessee

As warm and welcoming as a Christmas wreath, this cheery cherry coffee ring is delicious and drizzled with a pretty pink glaze. My family insists I make it for the Yuletide season.

    1 package (1/4 ounce) active dry yeast
    1 cup warm milk (110° to 115°)
    1 egg, lightly beaten
  1/4 cup sugar
  1/4 cup shortening
  3/4 teaspoon salt
3-1/2 to 4 cups all-purpose flour
  12 maraschino cherries, chopped and patted dry
FILLING:
  2/3 cup graham cracker crumbs (about 10 squares)
  3/4 cup packed brown sugar
  1/3 cup butter, melted
GLAZE:
    1 cup confectioners' sugar
  1/4 teaspoon almond extract
    6 to 8 teaspoons maraschino cherry juice

In a large mixing bowl, dissolve yeast in warm milk. Add the egg, sugar, shortening, salt and 2 cups flour; beat until smooth. Stir in cherries and enough remaining flour to form a soft dough.

Turn onto a lightly floured surface; knead until smooth and elastic, about 6-8 minutes. Place in a greased bowl, turning once to grease top. Cover and let rise in a warm place until doubled, about 1 hour.

Punch dough down. Turn onto a floured surface; roll into an 18-in. x 12-in. rectangle. Combine the filling ingredients until crumbly; sprinkle over dough. Roll up jelly-roll style, starting with a long side; pinch seam to seal. Place seam side down on a greased baking sheet; pinch ends together to form a ring. Cover and let rise in a warm place until doubled, about 45 minutes.

Bake at 375° for 23-28 minutes or until golden brown. Carefully remove from pan to a wire rack to cool. For glaze, combine the sugar, extract and enough juice to achieve drizzling consistency. Drizzle over cooled bread. **Yield:** 1 loaf.

MARMALADE MUFFINS
Phyllis Schmalz, Kansas City, Kansas

This is simply my all-time favorite recipe! The sweet orange marmalade added to the icing and baked right into these golden muffins makes breakfast something to celebrate.

    2 cups all-purpose flour
    3 tablespoons sugar
    2 teaspoons baking powder
3/4 teaspoon salt
    2 eggs
3/4 cup milk
2/3 cup orange marmalade
1/4 cup vegetable oil
ICING:
1/4 cup orange marmalade
    3 tablespoons cream cheese, softened
    1 cup confectioners' sugar

In a large bowl, combine the flour, sugar, baking powder and salt. In another bowl, beat the eggs, milk, marmalade and oil. Stir into dry ingredients just until moistened.

    Fill greased or paper-lined muffin cups three-fourths full. Bake at 350° for 18-20 minutes or until a toothpick comes out clean. Cool for 5 minutes before removing from pan to a wire rack.

    In a small mixing bowl, beat the marmalade and cream cheese until fluffy. Stir in confectioners' sugar until smooth. Spread over cooled muffins. Store in the refrigerator. **Yield:** 1 dozen.

PECAN CRANBERRY COFFEE CAKE
Ruth Francoeur, Adrian, Michigan

Yogurt and cranberry sauce make this colorful coffee cake extra moist and extra special! Serve it with coffee while opening gifts in the morning, with hot chocolate for a merry afternoon snack or even as a Christmas dessert.

1/2 cup butter, softened
    1 cup sugar
    2 eggs
    1 cup (8 ounces) plain yogurt
    1 teaspoon vanilla extract
    2 cups all-purpose flour
    1 teaspoon baking powder
    1 teaspoon baking soda
1/4 teaspoon salt
    1 can (16 ounces) whole-berry cranberry sauce,
      drained
TOPPING:
    1 cup chopped pecans
1/3 cup packed brown sugar
1/4 cup sugar
    1 teaspoon ground cinnamon

In a large mixing bowl, cream butter and sugar. Add eggs, one at a time, beating well after each addition. Combine the yogurt and vanilla. Combine the flour, baking powder, baking soda and salt; gradually add to the creamed mixture alternately with yogurt mixture.

    Set aside 1-1/2 cups batter; pour remaining batter into a greased 11-in. x 7-in. x 2-in. baking dish. Top with half of the cranberry sauce. Combine topping ingredients; sprinkle half over cranberry sauce. Top with reserved batter and remaining cranberry sauce and topping. Bake at 325° for 50-60 minutes or until a toothpick inserted near the center comes out clean. Cool on a wire rack. **Yield:** 9 servings.

TWISTER CHEDDAR ROLLS
Jane Birch, Edison, New Jersey
(Pictured below)

As flaky as homemade puff pastry, these buttery rolls bring compliments every time I serve them. Because they start with convenient refrigerated crescents, the mouth-watering treats couldn't be quicker or easier for busy holiday cooks!

    2 tubes (8 ounces *each*) refrigerated crescent rolls
1-1/2 cups (6 ounces) shredded cheddar cheese
1/4 cup chopped green onions
    1 egg
    1 teaspoon water
    2 teaspoons sesame seeds
1/2 teaspoon garlic salt *or* garlic powder
1/4 teaspoon dried parsley flakes

Separate crescent roll dough into eight rectangles; press seams to seal. Combine cheese and onions; spoon about 3 rounded tablespoonfuls lengthwise down the center of each rectangle to within 1/4 in. of each end. Fold dough in half lengthwise; firmly press edges to seal. Twist each strip four to five times. Bring ends together to form a ring; pinch to seal. Place on a greased baking sheet.

    In a small bowl, beat egg and water. Brush over dough. Combine the sesame seeds, garlic salt and parsley; sprinkle over rings. Bake at 375° for 14-16 minutes or until golden brown. Remove to wire racks; cool for 5 minutes before serving. **Yield:** 8 rolls.

Goodies for Gifts

Wrap up the season's best with tasty presents from your pantry. Friends and family will delight in merry morsels, snack mixes, spreads and breads.

BRIGHT BUTTER PASTRIES
Rosemary Browning, Symsonia, Kentucky
(Pictured on page 22)

I like to make these pretty pastries for the holidays. They take some time but are worth every buttery bite!

> 2 packages (1/4 ounce *each*) active dry yeast
> 1/4 cup warm water (110° to 115°)
> 1 cup warm milk (110° to 115°)
> 1/3 cup sugar
> 2 eggs
> 1/8 teaspoon salt
> 4 to 4-1/2 cups all-purpose flour
> 1 cup cold butter

FILLING:
> 1/4 cup packed brown sugar
> 1/4 cup chopped walnuts
> 1/4 teaspoon ground cinnamon
> 2 tablespoons butter, melted

Apple and cherry pie filling

GLAZE:
> 1 cup confectioners' sugar
> 2 tablespoons butter, softened
> 2 tablespoons evaporated milk
> 1/2 teaspoon vanilla extract

In a large mixing bowl, dissolve yeast in warm water. Add the milk, sugar, eggs, salt and 2 cups flour; beat until smooth. Stir in enough remaining flour to form a soft dough. Do not knead. Cover and refrigerate for 15 minutes.

Turn dough onto a lightly floured surface. Roll into an 18-in. x 15-in. rectangle. Cut 1/3 cup butter into small pieces. Dot dough with butter to within 1 in. of edges. Fold lengthwise into thirds, then widthwise into thirds, forming a 6-in. x 5-in. rectangle. Wrap in plastic wrap; refrigerate for 15 minutes. Repeat the rolling, dotting with butter, folding and chilling two times.

Turn onto a lightly floured surface; divide dough in half. For fans, combine the brown sugar, walnuts and cinnamon; set aside. Roll one portion of dough into an 18-in. x 10-in. rectangle. Cut into eighteen 5-in. x 2-in. rectangles. Brush with melted butter to within 1/2 in. of edges; sprinkle with brown sugar mixture. Roll up jelly-roll style, starting with a long side; pinch seams to seal. Place seam side down on a greased baking sheet; curve ends down to form crescent shape. With scissors, cut from outside edge to two-thirds of the way toward opposite side at 1-in. intervals. Cover and let rise until doubled, about 1 hour.

For S-shaped rolls, divide other portion of dough into 18 pieces. Shape each piece into a 10-in. rope. Shape rope into an S shape, then coil ends until they touch the center. Place 2 in. apart on a greased baking sheet. Fill coil ends with 1-2 teaspoons pie filling. Cover and let rise until doubled, about 1 hour.

Bake at 375° for 8-10 minutes or until golden brown. Re-

GIFTS OF GOOD TASTE. Everyone on your list is sure to enjoy delicious Bright Butter Pastries, Cajun Party Mix and zesty Jalapeno Pepper Jelly (p. 22, clockwise from lower right).

move from pans to wire racks to cool. In a small bowl, combine the glaze ingredients. Drizzle over rolls. **Yield:** 3 dozen.

CAJUN PARTY MIX
Twila Burkholder, Middleburg, Pennsylvania
(Pictured on page 22)

I pack this mix in Christmas tins to give to friends and family. They can't seem to get enough—and it's so easy!

> 6 cups miniature fish-shaped crackers
> 6 cups pretzel sticks
> 3 cups Rice Chex
> 3 cups Corn Chex
> 1 can (11-1/2 ounces) mixed nuts
> 1 cup butter, melted
> 1 teaspoon garlic powder
> 1/2 to 1 teaspoon celery salt
> 1/2 teaspoon cayenne pepper
> 1/8 teaspoon hot pepper sauce

In a large roasting pan, combine the first five ingredients. Combine the butter, garlic powder, celery salt, cayenne and hot pepper sauce; pour over cereal mixture and stir to coat. Bake, uncovered, at 250° for 35-40 minutes, stirring every 15 minutes. Cool completely. Store in airtight containers. **Yield:** about 5 quarts.

JALAPENO PEPPER JELLY
Bev Elliott, Peotone, Illinois
(Pictured on page 22)

My family relishes this jelly served with meat or spread on crackers with cream cheese. It's in hot demand as a gift.

> 5 cups sugar
> 2 medium tart apples, peeled and coarsely chopped

1-1/2 cups cider vinegar
> 3/4 cup finely chopped green pepper
> 8 to 10 jalapeno peppers, seeded and chopped*
> 1/4 cup water
> 6 to 8 drops green food coloring
> 2 pouches (3 ounces *each*) liquid fruit pectin

Cream cheese and assorted crackers

In a large saucepan, combine the sugar, apples, vinegar, green pepper, jalapenos and water. Bring to a boil. Reduce heat; simmer, uncovered, for 10 minutes. Strain mixture and return to pan. Stir in food coloring. Return to a rolling boil over high heat. Stir in pectin; boil for 2 minutes, stirring constantly.

Remove from the heat; skim off foam. Pour hot liquid into sterilized jars, leaving 1/4-in. headspace. Adjust caps. Process for 10 minutes in a boiling-water bath. Serve with cream cheese on crackers. **Yield:** about 5 half-pints.

*Editor's Note: When cutting or seeding hot peppers, use rubber or plastic gloves to protect your hands. Avoid touching your face.

GINGER HONEY MUSTARD
Lynne Ellis, Lawrence, Kansas

This mustard makes a tangy stocking stuffer. We've found it tastes great with meats…and pretzels, too!

- 1/2 cup Dijon mustard
- 1/4 cup honey
- 3/4 teaspoon ground ginger *or* 1 tablespoon finely chopped fresh gingerroot
- 1 teaspoon lemon juice
- 1 teaspoon vegetable oil

In a food processor or blender, combine all ingredients; cover and process until smooth. Transfer to a jar or container. Refrigerate for 2 hours before serving. Store in the refrigerator. **Yield:** about 3/4 cup.

BAKE 'N' TAKE LITTLE FRUITCAKES
C.M. Purdy, Stevensville, Michigan

Even folks who don't like traditional fruitcake savor these muffin-size treats. I enjoy the recipe because it's so easy.

- 3/4 cup all-purpose flour
- 3/4 cup sugar
- 1/2 teaspoon baking powder
- 1/2 teaspoon salt
- 3 eggs, lightly beaten
- 1 package (16 ounces) pecan pieces
- 1 package (16 ounces) pitted dates, coarsely chopped
- 1-1/2 cups coarsely chopped dried apricots
- 1 cup dried cranberries *or* cherries
- 3/4 cup coarsely chopped dried plums
- 3/4 cup coarsely chopped dried apples
- 3/4 cup coarsely chopped dried peaches, nectarines *or* mixed fruit

In a large bowl, combine the flour, sugar, baking powder and salt; stir in eggs just until moistened. Fold in the remaining ingredients. Fill greased muffin cups. Bake at 325° for 20-25 minutes or until set. Cool for 10 minutes before removing from pans to wire racks to cool completely. Store in an airtight container. **Yield:** about 2-1/2 dozen.

SWEET POTATO MINI LOAVES
Trish Kent, Merritt Island, Florida

Here's a wonderful present for drop-in visitors, the kids' teachers or neighbors. One batch makes six adorable mini loaves—and you might add some butter or cream cheese for an extra-special present.

- 4 eggs
- 2 cups sugar
- 2 cups cold mashed sweet potatoes
- 3/4 cup vegetable oil
- 2 cups all-purpose flour
- 1-1/2 cups whole wheat flour
- 1-1/2 teaspoons ground cinnamon
- 1 teaspoon baking soda
- 1 teaspoon ground nutmeg
- 1/2 teaspoon salt
- 2/3 cup water

In a large mixing bowl, beat the eggs, sugar, sweet potatoes and oil. Combine the flours, cinnamon, baking soda, nutmeg and salt; add to sweet potato mixture alternately with water.

Pour into six greased 5-3/4-in. x 3-in. x 2-in. loaf pans. Bake at 350° for 30-35 minutes or until a toothpick inserted near the center comes out clean. Cool for 10 minutes before removing from pans to wire racks. **Yield:** 6 mini loaves.

PRALINE PECANS
Dana Campbell, Gordon, Texas

With pecans so plentiful in Texas, these sweet crunchy nuts have become an expected tradition. Everyone in my family asks me to make them again and again for festive gatherings.

- 1 cup sugar
- 1 cup packed brown sugar
- 1/2 cup water
- 2 tablespoons honey
- 1/2 teaspoon ground cinnamon
- 3 teaspoons vanilla extract
- 1/4 teaspoon rum extract
- 3 cups pecan halves

In a heavy saucepan, combine the sugars, water, honey and cinnamon. Bring to a boil over medium heat; do not stir. Cook over medium heat until a candy thermometer reads 240° (soft-ball stage). Remove from the heat; add extracts. Cool to lukewarm without stirring.

Beat with a mixer for 2-3 minutes or until creamy. Stir in pecans until coated. Turn onto waxed paper (mixture will be sticky); separate large clumps. Cool for several hours or until dry and sugary. Store in an airtight container. **Yield:** 3 cups.

RUSSIAN TEA
Lois Hill, Bethlehem, Pennsylvania

Friends will appreciate your thoughtfulness every time they sip this tasty tea. Red-hots add a spicy seasonal touch to this easy-to-make gift mix.

- 2 cups orange breakfast drink mix
- 2 cups sugar
- 1 cup unsweetened instant tea
- 1 envelope (.23 ounce) unsweetened lemonade soft drink mix
- 1 teaspoon ground cinnamon
- 1 teaspoon ground cloves
- 1/3 cup red-hot candies
- **ADDITIONAL INGREDIENT (for each serving):**
- 1 cup boiling water

In a bowl, combine the first seven ingredients. Store in an airtight container in a cool dry place for up to 6 months. **Yield:** about 4-1/4 cups.

To prepare hot tea: Place 2 teaspoons tea mix in a mug; stir in boiling water until mix is dissolved. **Yield:** 1 serving.

CRANBERRY NUT BARK
Betty Richardson, Walnut Cove, North Carolina
(Pictured above)

Studded with chunks of cranberries and nuts, this sweet creamy confection is the perfect last-minute gift! It's ready to wrap in less than 30 minutes, and everyone who tries it asks for more—and requests the recipe, too.

    1 pound white candy coating, coarsely chopped
    1 cup dried cranberries
    1 cup coarsely chopped macadamia nuts *or* pistachios, toasted

In a large microwave-safe bowl, melt candy coating at 70% power for 1 minute; stir. Microwave at 30-second intervals, stirring until smooth. Stir in cranberries and nuts. Spread onto a waxed paper-lined baking sheet. Refrigerate for 20 minutes. Break into small pieces; store in airtight containers. **Yield:** about 1-3/4 pounds.

Editor's Note: This recipe was tested in a 1,100-watt microwave.

CHERRY HAZELNUT BISCOTTI
Ruth Lee, Troy, Ontario

Presents from the pantry are a tradition with me—and this crusty coffee "dunker" is a favorite! Stuffed with fruit and nuts, it freezes well and can be made a month ahead of busy holidays. Dried cranberries can be substituted for cherries.

    4 cups all-purpose flour
    1 cup chopped hazelnuts, toasted
    1 tablespoon grated lemon peel
    2 teaspoons baking powder
    1/2 teaspoon salt
    4 eggs
1-1/3 cups sugar
    1/2 cup vegetable oil
    1 tablespoon lemon juice
    1 teaspoon vanilla extract
    1 cup dried cherries *or* cranberries

In a large bowl, combine the first five ingredients. In another bowl, whisk the eggs; add the sugar, oil, lemon juice and vanilla. Add to the dry ingredients just until combined. Stir in cherries. Divide dough in half.

On a parchment-lined baking sheet, shape each portion into a 12-in. x 3-in. rectangle. Bake at 325° for 30-35 minutes or until lightly browned. Carefully remove to wire racks; cool for 5 minutes. Reduce oven temperature to 300°.

Transfer biscotti to a cutting board; cut diagonally with a serrated knife into 3/4-in. slices. Place cut side down on parchment-lined baking sheets. Bake for 25-35 minutes or until firm, turning after 15 minutes. Remove to wire racks to cool. Store in an airtight container. **Yield:** about 2-1/2 dozen.

CINNAMON WALNUT BRITTLE
Julie Radcliffe, Butte, Montana

Seasoned with cinnamon, this spicy brittle is a great gift or family snack to munch while watching Christmas movies. Best of all, it goes together quick as a wink in the microwave.

    1 cup sugar
    1/2 cup light corn syrup
    1 cup chopped walnuts
    1 teaspoon butter
    1/2 teaspoon ground cinnamon
    1 teaspoon baking soda
    1 teaspoon vanilla extract

Butter a baking sheet; set aside. In a 2-qt. microwave-safe bowl, combine sugar and corn syrup. Microwave, uncovered, on high for 3 minutes; stir. Cook, uncovered, on high 2-1/2 minutes longer. Stir in walnuts, butter and cinnamon. Microwave, uncovered, on high for 2 minutes or until mixture turns a light amber color (mixture will be very hot). Quickly stir in baking soda and vanilla until light and foamy. Immediately pour onto prepared pan; spread with a metal spatula. Cool; break into pieces. **Yield:** 3/4 pound.

Editor's Note: This recipe was tested in a 1,100-watt microwave.

CARAMEL NUT CRUNCH
Mary Sweere, Hilbert, Wisconsin

I discovered this crispy snack recipe on a box of cereal years ago. It's been a Christmas favorite with my friends and family ever since.

    1/2 cup packed brown sugar
    1/2 cup corn syrup
    1/4 cup butter
    1/2 teaspoon salt
    4 cups Cheerios
    1 cup pecan halves
    1 cup walnut halves
    1 cup salted dry roasted peanuts
    1 cup whole unblanched almonds

In a saucepan, heat the brown sugar, corn syrup, butter and salt over medium heat for 5 minutes or until sugar is dissolved, stirring constantly.

In a large heatproof bowl, combine the remaining ingredients. Pour hot syrup over cereal mixture; stir until well coated. Spread into a greased 15-in. x 10-in. x 1-in. baking pan. Bake at 300° for 30 minutes or until crisp, stirring every 10 minutes. Cool on a wire rack until slightly firm. **Yield:** 8 cups.

Sugarplum Sweets

Satisfy your family's holiday sweet tooth with a finger-licking legacy of Christmas confections and scrumptious once-a-year munchies.

PEANUT CANDY LOGS
Marilee Braesch, Omaha, Nebraska
(Pictured on page 26)

These caramel-topped logs with sweet nougat centers take a little extra effort to make—but candy this festive is worth it for the holidays!

    1 jar (7 ounces) marshmallow creme
    2 tablespoons milk, *divided*
    1 teaspoon vanilla extract
    4 cups confectioners' sugar
    1 pound caramels (about 75)
    2 cups salted dry roasted peanuts, finely chopped

In a large mixing bowl, combine the marshmallow creme, 1 tablespoon milk and vanilla. Gradually beat in confectioners' sugar until combined. With lightly greased hands, shape the mixture into 1-1/2-in. x 3/4-in. logs. Place on a waxed paper-lined baking sheet. Freeze for 3-4 hours or until firm.

Place the caramels and remaining milk in a microwave-safe bowl. Microwave, uncovered, at 70% power for 1 minute. Stir; heat 1 to 1-1/2 minutes longer or until mixture is melted and blended.

Remove four logs from the freezer at a time. Pierce with a meat fork and spoon caramel over all sides. Shake or scrape off excess caramel. Immediately roll in peanuts. Place on waxed paper. Repeat with remaining logs. Reheat caramel in the microwave for 15 seconds as needed. Store in an airtight container in the refrigerator. **Yield:** 3 dozen.

Editor's Note: This recipe was tested with Hershey caramels in a 1,100-watt microwave.

HOMEMADE GUMDROPS
Christin Holt, Kingsburg, California
(Pictured on page 26)

Your friends and family will remember these chewy fruity candies long after they've licked the last bit of sugar off their fingers! They're a great gift any time of year.

2-1/2 cups sugar, *divided*
1-1/3 cups applesauce
    2 packages (3 ounces *each*) red *or* green gelatin
    2 envelopes unflavored gelatin
    1 teaspoon lemon juice

In a large saucepan, combine 2 cups sugar, applesauce, red or green gelatin, unflavored gelatin and lemon juice; let stand for 1 minute. Bring to a boil over medium heat, stirring constantly. Boil for 1 minute. Immediately pour into a cold 11-in. x 7-in. x 2-in. pan coated with nonstick cooking spray. Refrigerate for 3 hours or until firm.

SWEET SENSATIONS to mark the Yuletide season include sweet-salty Peanut Candy Logs, creamy chocolate-covered Maple Nut Balls and sugar-dusted red and green Homemade Gumdrops (p. 26, clockwise from lower left).

With a spatula, loosen gelatin from sides of pan. To remove, invert onto waxed paper. Using kitchen scissors or small sharp cookie cutters dipped in hot water, cut into 1-in. squares or shapes. Place on waxed paper. Dry at room temperature for about 8 hours or until slightly sticky. Roll in remaining sugar. Store in an airtight container. **Yield:** about 1-3/4 pounds.

MAPLE NUT BALLS
Kathryn Jackson, Benson, North Carolina
(Pictured on page 26)

I created these chocolate-dipped delights a few years ago, and already they've become a seasonal favorite with all my friends and family members. The creamy confections also won a blue ribbon at our state fair.

    1/2 cup butter, softened
    2 teaspoons maple flavoring
3-1/2 cups confectioners' sugar
    1 cup finely chopped pecans
    1 package (11-1/2 ounces) milk chocolate chips
    2 teaspoons shortening

In a mixing bowl, cream butter and maple flavoring. Add confectioners' sugar; mix well. Beat in pecans. Shape into 1-in. balls. Cover and refrigerate for 1-1/2 hours or until firm. In a heavy saucepan or microwave, melt chocolate chips and shortening; stir until smooth. Dip balls in chocolate mixture. Place on waxed paper until set. Store in the refrigerator. **Yield:** about 3-1/2 dozen.

COCONUT DATE BALLS
Sharol Millard, Harrisonville, Missouri

There are a few classic recipes I absolutely have to pull out every Christmas, and this is one of those. These chewy balls are surprisingly crunchy and they look so pretty on a holiday candy tray.

    1/2 cup butter
    1 cup chopped dates
3/4 cup sugar
    2 eggs, beaten
    1 cup chopped pecans
    1 cup crisp rice cereal
    1 teaspoon vanilla extract
    2 cups flaked coconut

In a saucepan, melt butter over low heat. Stir in the dates, sugar and eggs. Cook and stir over low heat for 10-15 minutes or until a thermometer reads 160°. Remove from the heat; stir in the pecans, cereal and vanilla. When cool enough to handle, shape into 1-in. balls; roll in coconut. Place on waxed paper-lined baking sheets. Refrigerate for 1-2 hours or until firm. Store in an airtight container in the refrigerator. **Yield:** about 5 dozen.

caramels and 10 tablespoons butter in another saucepan; cook and stir over low heat until melted. Stir in the milk until smooth. Cool for 10 minutes; pour over cereal layer. Refrigerate for about 30 minutes or until firm.

In a large saucepan, melt the remaining butter and marshmallows. Stir in remaining cereal. Spread over caramel layer. Cover and refrigerate for 30 minutes or until firm. Cut into bars. Store in the refrigerator. **Yield:** 2-1/2 dozen.

*Editor's Note: This recipe was tested with Hershey caramels.

SURPRISE FUDGE
Linda Allard, Freeport, Maine

Santa himself would never guess that the secret ingredient in this amazingly smooth and creamy fudge is cheese! The recipe is simply delicious and is my husband's Yuletide favorite.

> 8 ounces process cheese (Velveeta), cubed
> 3/4 cup unsalted butter, cubed
> 1 teaspoon vanilla extract
> 1 cup chopped nuts
> 3-3/4 cups confectioners' sugar
> 1/2 cup baking cocoa

In a saucepan, cook and stir the cheese and butter over medium heat until melted. Remove from the heat; stir in the vanilla and nuts. In a mixing bowl, combine the confectioners' sugar and cocoa. Add the cheese mixture and beat until combined (mixture will be stiff). Spread into a greased 9-in. square pan. Refrigerate until firm. Cut into squares. Store in the refrigerator. **Yield:** about 2 pounds.

TOOTSIE ROLL FUDGE
Carolyn McDill, Ohatchee, Alabama

When my husband came home with 50 pounds of Tootsie Rolls he bought at a discount store, I had to figure out a way to use them—so I came up with this recipe! A red or green M&M atop each piece makes them extra jolly.

> 1 teaspoon plus 2 tablespoons butter, *divided*
> 2 cups miniature Tootsie Rolls
> 2 tablespoons peanut butter
> 3-3/4 cups confectioners' sugar
> 2 tablespoons milk
> 1 teaspoon vanilla extract
> 1 cup chopped pecans
> 1/3 cup green and red M&M's

Line a 9-in. square pan with foil. Grease the foil with 1 teaspoon butter; set aside. In a heavy saucepan, melt the Tootsie Rolls, peanut butter and remaining butter over low heat, stirring constantly. Gradually stir in the confectioners' sugar, milk and vanilla (mixture will be very thick). Fold in pecans.

Spread into prepared pan. Using a sharp knife, score the surface into 1-in. squares. Press an M&M into the center of each square. Cool. Using foil, remove fudge from pan; cut into squares. Store in an airtight container. **Yield:** about 2 pounds.

EASY CHOCOLATE TRUFFLES
Denise Doig, Walkerton, Indiana
(Pictured above)

My children and I often make these super-easy chocolate balls during the holiday season to dress up our cookie trays and gift baskets. For added color, the balls can be rolled in nonpareils, sprinkles or ground nuts.

> 4 cups (24 ounces) semisweet chocolate chips
> 1 can (14 ounces) sweetened condensed milk
> 1/2 teaspoon almond extract
> 1/8 teaspoon salt
> Colored nonpareils and sprinkles

In a microwave or heavy saucepan, melt chocolate chips; stir until smooth. Stir in the milk, almond extract and salt. Cool to room temperature. Shape into 1-in. balls; roll in nonpareils and sprinkles. Store in an airtight container. **Yield:** about 6 dozen (about 2-1/4 pounds).

CRISPY CARAMEL TREATS
Marlis Asprey, West Sacto, California

Kids love these triple-decker treats for the holidays—or any time at all. I always make several batches because my neighbors can't seem to get enough of them.

> 1/2 cup plus 10 tablespoons butter, *divided*
> 8 cups miniature marshmallows, *divided*
> 8 cups crisp rice cereal, *divided*
> 1 package (14 ounces) caramels*
> 1 can (14 ounces) sweetened condensed milk

In a large saucepan, melt 1/4 cup butter and 4 cups marshmallows. Stir in 4 cups cereal. Pat into a greased 13-in. x 9-in. x 2-in. pan; set aside. For caramel filling, place the

CORN CHIP CRUNCH
Nancy Schreur, Zeeland, Michigan

Folks can't seem to stop eating this sweet and salty treat when I serve it. A nice twist on popcorn or cereal snack mixes, it's great for munching on during holiday movies and parades or football games.

    6 cups corn chips
1-1/2 cups dry roasted peanuts
  1/2 cup packed brown sugar
  1/2 cup dark corn syrup
  1/4 cup butter

In a large heatproof bowl, combine corn chips and peanuts. In a small saucepan, combine the brown sugar, corn syrup and butter. Bring to a boil over medium heat, stirring constantly. Pour over corn chip mixture; toss to coat. Transfer to a greased 15-in. x 10-in. x 1-in. baking pan. Bake at 250° for 30-40 minutes, stirring every 15 minutes. Spread onto waxed paper; cool. Break apart and store in airtight containers. **Yield:** 8 cups.

WHITE CHOCOLATE CEREAL CLUSTERS
Marge Gregorash, Erickson, Manitoba

Just three ingredients and 3 minutes in the microwave are all it takes to make the season bright with this sweet treat.

    4 cups Golden Grahams cereal
1-1/2 cups honey roasted peanuts
    2 cups vanilla *or* white chips

In a large bowl, combine the cereal and peanuts. In a microwave-safe bowl, melt chips at 30% power for 3 minutes, stirring every minute until smooth. Pour over cereal mixture; stir until well coated. Spread onto a waxed paper-lined baking sheet. Let stand until chocolate is set. Break into small pieces. **Yield:** about 6 cups.

   Editor's Note: This recipe was tested in a 1,100-watt microwave oven.

CHOCOLATE BUGLES
Penny Roberts, Memphis, Tennessee

This is my most-requested Christmas candy. Each December, my husband, daughter and I whip up batches to fill colorful tins that we give to all our friends. It's so easy and fun to make!

1-1/2 cups creamy peanut butter
    6 cups original flavor Bugles
   12 ounces milk chocolate candy coating

Cut a small hole in the corner of a plastic bag; fill bag with peanut butter. Pipe the peanut butter into the Bugles. In a microwave-safe bowl, melt candy coating at 70% power for 1-1/2 minutes; stir. Heat 1 to 1-1/2 minutes longer or until melted; stir until smooth. Dip the filled end of Bugles halfway in coating. Place on waxed paper to dry. **Yield:** about 14 dozen.

   Editor's Note: This recipe was tested in a 1,100-watt microwave oven.

PEANUT BUTTERCREAM CANDY
Ann Bergmann, Saint Augustine, Florida

My cousin sent me some of these delicious nutty buttercreams, and I've been making them ever since. It's a wonderful gift recipe since one batch yields seven dozen.

    1 cup butter, softened
7-1/2 cups confectioners' sugar
    2 tablespoons half-and-half cream
    1 teaspoon vanilla extract
    3 cups milk chocolate chips
    2 teaspoons shortening
2-1/2 cups finely chopped peanuts

In a large mixing bowl, cream the butter. Gradually add confectioners' sugar, cream and vanilla; beat on medium speed for 3-4 minutes. Shape into 3/4-in. balls. In a microwave or heavy saucepan, melt chocolate chips and shortening; stir until smooth. Dip balls in melted chocolate; roll in peanuts. Place on waxed paper-lined baking sheets; refrigerate until firm. Store in an airtight container in the refrigerator. **Yield:** about 7 dozen.

BUTTER ALMOND CRUNCH
Judy Hamilton, Charleston, West Virginia

I always draw rave reviews for this buttery, melt-in-your-mouth candy. From the coconut bottom layer to the chocolate drizzled on top, it's a winner all year-round.

1-1/2 teaspoons plus 1/2 cup butter, *divided*
  3/4 cup flaked coconut
1-1/2 cups sugar
    3 tablespoons water
    1 tablespoon light corn syrup
  3/4 cup sliced almonds
  1/2 cup semisweet chocolate chips

Line a 13-in. x 9-in. x 2-in. pan with foil. Grease the foil with 1-1/2 teaspoons butter. Spread coconut evenly into prepared pan; set aside. In a heavy saucepan, combine the sugar, water and corn syrup. Bring to a boil over medium heat, stirring occasionally. Add remaining butter; cook and stir until butter is melted. Continue cooking, without stirring, until a candy thermometer reads 300° (hard-crack stage). Remove from the heat. Stir in almonds. Pour over coconut. Cool.

   In a microwave or heavy saucepan, melt chocolate chips; stir until smooth. Drizzle over candy; cool until firm. Remove from foil and break into pieces. Store in airtight containers. **Yield:** about 1-1/4 pounds.

Candy Thermometers
'TIS the season for using candy thermometers, so here's a helpful tip:

● We recommend that you test your candy thermometer before each use by bringing water to a boil; the thermometer should read 212°. Adjust your recipe temperature up or down based on your test.

Appetizers

Set everyone's holiday spirits stirring with a wondrous spread of fun finger foods, hearty party snacks and tempting Yuletide treats.

HOLIDAY SANDWICH WREATH
Ginger George Gentry, Sutherlin, Virginia
(Pictured on page 30)

This jolly sandwich wreath always disappears in a twinkling at parties! Best of all, I can put it together in no time using deli ham and chicken salads—or sometimes I make my own. Try decking it with "holly" fashioned from parsley and grape tomatoes.

  1/4 cup butter, softened
   20 slices snack rye bread
   20 slices snack pumpernickel bread
HAM SALAD:
  1/2 pound deli ham salad
  1/4 cup finely chopped celery
  1/2 teaspoon Worcestershire sauce
CHICKEN SALAD:
  1/2 pound deli chicken salad
  1/4 cup diced peeled apple
   1 tablespoon sour cream
Christmas ribbon bow, optional

Spread butter over one side of each slice of bread. In a bowl, combine the ham salad ingredients. In another bowl, combine the chicken salad, apple and sour cream. Spread ham salad on half of the rye bread slices; top with remaining rye. Spread chicken salad on half of the pumpernickel bread slices; top with remaining pumpernickel. Arrange sandwiches in a circle on a serving plate. Decorate with a bow if desired. **Yield: 20 sandwiches.**

CHEDDAR ARTICHOKE QUICHE CUPS
Fran Dell, Las Vegas, Nevada
(Pictured on page 30)

Santa himself couldn't resist sampling these savory bites chock-full of artichokes, onions and cheese. They're at the top of my family's list for every holiday gathering. And whether I serve them hot or cold, there are never any left!

   2 jars (7-1/2 ounces *each*) marinated artichoke hearts
   1 small onion, finely chopped
   1 garlic clove, minced
   4 eggs, beaten
  1/4 cup dry bread crumbs
  1/4 teaspoon ground mustard
  1/8 teaspoon dried oregano
  1/8 teaspoon pepper
  1/8 teaspoon hot pepper sauce
   2 cups (8 ounces) shredded cheddar cheese
   2 tablespoons minced fresh parsley

Drain artichokes, reserving half of the marinade. Chop artichokes; set aside. In a skillet, saute onion and garlic in re-

served marinade until tender; set aside. In a large bowl, combine the eggs, bread crumbs, mustard, oregano, pepper and hot pepper sauce. Stir in the cheese, parsley, reserved artichokes and onion mixture.

Fill miniature muffin cups three-fourths full. Bake at 325° for 15-17 minutes or until set. Cool for 5 minutes before removing from pan to wire racks. Serve warm. Refrigerate leftovers. **Yield: 4 dozen.**

CHRISTMAS PIZZA STRIPS
Margaret Pache, Mesa, Arizona
(Pictured on page 30)

Looking to add a dash of Christmas color to your appetizer mix? Topped with roasted peppers, caramelized onions, beef and black olives, this popular pizza is as tasty as it is decorative on the table.

   2 tablespoons butter
   1 tablespoon vegetable oil
   1 large onion, thinly sliced
  1/2 cup sugar
   1 pound ground beef
  1/2 teaspoon salt
  1/8 teaspoon pepper
   1 tablespoon cornmeal
   1 tube (10 ounces) refrigerated pizza crust
1-1/2 cups (6 ounces) shredded mozzarella cheese
   1 jar (7 ounces) roasted red peppers, drained and sliced
   1 medium tomato, seeded and diced
  1/2 cup sliced ripe olives

In a nonstick skillet, heat butter and oil; add onion and sugar. Cook and stir over low heat for 30-35 minutes or until onion is caramelized. In another skillet, cook beef over medium heat until no longer pink; drain. Sprinkle with salt and pepper; set aside.

Sprinkle cornmeal into a greased 13-in. x 9-in. x 2-in. baking pan. Press pizza dough into pan; prick dough with a fork. Bake at 400° for 10 minutes. Top with the beef, caramelized onion, cheese, red peppers, tomato and olives. Bake 10-12 minutes longer or until cheese is melted. **Yield: 15 servings.**

WHEN SETTING UP appetizers, it can be a challenge to have everything ready at the same time. Try these tips to smooth out service:
  ● To make preparation and holiday entertaining easier, serve both hot last-minute appetizers with cold do-ahead treats.
  ● Remember to allow cheese balls, dips and spreads that contain cream cheese to stand out at room temperature 15 minutes before serving—they'll spread more easily and have more flavor.

ENTERTAINING APPETIZERS. Get your party off to a great start with a Holiday Sandwich Wreath, Cheddar Artichoke Quiche Cups and Christmas Pizza Strips (p. 30, from top to bottom).

TIERED CHEESE SLICES

Diane Benjaminson, Coleville, Saskatchewan
(Pictured above)

I can't tell you how many times I've made this recipe or been asked to share it! Guests always think I fussed, but the simple ingredients go together in minutes using pre-sliced cheese. For busy holiday hostesses, it's a do-ahead delight.

    1 package (8 ounces) cream cheese, softened
1/2 teaspoon hot pepper sauce
1/4 teaspoon salt
1/4 cup finely chopped pecans
1/4 cup finely chopped dried cranberries
    2 packages (8 ounces *each*) deli-style cheddar
       cheese slices* (about 3 inches square)
Assorted crackers

In a small mixing bowl, combine the cream cheese, hot pepper sauce and salt. Stir in pecans and cranberries. On a 12-in. square of aluminum foil, place two slices of cheese side by side; spread with 2-3 tablespoons cream cheese mixture. Repeat layers six times. Top with two cheese slices. (Save remaining cheese slices for another use.)

   Fold foil around cheese and seal tightly. Refrigerate for 8 hours or overnight. Cut in half lengthwise and then widthwise into 1/4-in. slices. Serve with crackers. **Yield:** about 4 dozen.

   *Editor's Note: This recipe was tested with Sargento deli-style sharp cheddar cheese slices.

CRAB-STUFFED MUSHROOMS

Harriet Stichter, Milford, Indiana

Ever since I found this elegant recipe in a magazine years ago, these seafood-stuffed morsels have been making my family and friends merry every Christmas.

   36 large fresh mushrooms (about 3 pounds)
1/2 cup butter, *divided*
1-1/2 cups finely chopped onions
   3 cans (6 ounces *each*) crabmeat, drained, flaked
      and cartilage removed

   3 tablespoons lemon juice
1/2 cup mayonnaise
1/4 cup minced fresh parsley
   1 teaspoon Worcestershire sauce
1/2 teaspoon salt
1/4 teaspoon pepper
1/4 cup grated Parmesan cheese

Remove stems from mushrooms; set caps aside. Finely chop stems. In a skillet, melt 1/4 cup butter; saute stems and onions until tender. In a bowl, combine crab and lemon juice. Add the onion mixture, mayonnaise, parsley, Worcestershire sauce, salt and pepper; mix well.

   Stuff into mushroom caps; sprinkle with Parmesan cheese. Place in a greased 15-in. x 10-in. x 1-in. baking pan. Melt remaining butter; drizzle over mushrooms. Bake, uncovered, at 350° for 20-25 minutes or until heated through. Serve warm. **Yield:** 3 dozen.

CHICKEN-FRIED STEAK FINGERS

Barbara Radden, Belleville, Illinois

Christmas simply wouldn't be complete without these finger-licking good steak snacks. Two weeks before the holidays, I make and freeze a double batch to fry up for Christmas Eve supper or set out with dipping sauce and frilled party picks.

   2 eggs
   3 tablespoons milk
   2 cups seasoned bread crumbs
   1 teaspoon salt
1/2 teaspoon pepper
   1 beef flank steak (1-1/2 pounds), thinly sliced
Vegetable oil for frying
Barbecue sauce *or* ranch salad dressing

In a shallow bowl, beat eggs and milk. In another shallow bowl, combine the bread crumbs, salt and pepper. Dip steak strips into egg mixture, then roll in crumbs.

   In skillet, heat 2 tablespoons of oil. Fry strips, a few at a time, for 1-2 minutes on each side or until golden brown. Add oil as needed. Drain on paper towels. Serve with barbecue sauce or ranch dressing. **Yield:** about 4 dozen.

GOLDEN GLOW PUNCH

Bernice Knutson, Danbury, Iowa

Garnished with peach slices and dollops of ice cream, this frothy fruit punch is as pretty as the glow of Christmas candles! It adds a refreshing touch to any holiday buffet.

   3 cups apricot nectar, chilled
   1 can (6 ounces) frozen orange juice concentrate,
      thawed
   5 cups lemon-lime soda, chilled
   1 package (16 ounces) frozen sliced peaches,
      thawed
   1 cup vanilla ice cream

In a large bowl, combine the apricot nectar, orange juice concentrate and soda; mix well. Add the peaches. Top with small scoopfuls of ice cream. **Yield:** 9-12 servings.

MINI CHIMICHANGAS
Kathy Rogers, Hudson, Ohio

Wish your guests "Feliz Navidad" with this south-of-the-border specialty! Hearty enough to serve as a meal, these flavorful and filling wraps draw raves whenever I serve them.

- 1 pound ground beef
- 1 medium onion, chopped
- 1 envelope taco seasoning
- 3/4 cup water
- 3 cups (12 ounces) shredded Monterey Jack cheese
- 1 cup (8 ounces) sour cream
- 1 can (4 ounces) chopped green chilies, drained
- 1 package (1 pound) egg roll wrappers (14 count)
- 1 egg white, lightly beaten
- Vegetable oil for frying
- Salsa and additional sour cream

In a skillet, cook beef and onion over medium heat until meat is no longer pink; drain. Stir in taco seasoning and water. Bring to a boil. Reduce heat; simmer, uncovered, for 5 minutes, stirring occasionally. Remove from the heat; cool slightly.

In a bowl, combine the cheese, sour cream and chilies. Stir in beef mixture. Place an egg roll wrapper on work surface with one point facing you. Place 1/3 cup filling in center. Fold bottom third of wrapper over filling; fold in sides. Brush top point with egg white; roll up to seal. Repeat with remaining wrappers and filling. (Keep remaining egg roll wrappers covered with waxed paper to avoid drying out.)

In a large saucepan, heat 1 in. of oil to 375°. Fry chimichangas for 1-1/2 minutes on each side or until golden brown. Drain on paper towels. Serve warm with salsa and sour cream. **Yield:** 14 servings.

BLUE CHEESE GARLIC DIP
Lillian Nardi, Richmond, California

This thick, creamy dip is my mom's recipe and a family favorite for ringing in the season. It also makes a tasty substitute for mayonnaise on chicken and turkey sandwiches.

- 1/2 cup milk
- 1 package (8 ounces) cream cheese, cubed
- 1 cup (4 ounces) crumbled blue cheese
- 2 garlic cloves, peeled
- Assorted crackers

In a blender, combine the milk, cream cheese, blue cheese and garlic; cover and process until blended. Serve with crackers. **Yield:** about 1-1/2 cups.

CORNED BEEF ROLL-UPS
Mary June Mullins, Livonia, Missouri

Instead of buying gifts for extended family, we donate the money to a worthy cause, then exchange things we no longer use. This savory dish is the one I'm always asked to bring.

- 1 package (8 ounces) cream cheese, softened
- 1 tablespoon finely chopped onion
- 1 teaspoon Worcestershire sauce

- 1/8 teaspoon salt
- 1/8 teaspoon pepper
- Dash hot pepper sauce
- 2 packages (2-1/2 ounces *each*) deli corned beef
- Assorted crackers

In a large mixing bowl, beat cream cheese until smooth. Add the onion, Worcestershire sauce, salt, pepper and hot pepper sauce; mix well.

Place two slices of corned beef on waxed paper. Spread 2 teaspoons cream cheese mixture over each slice. Stack one slice of corned beef on top of the other. Roll up tightly; wrap in plastic wrap. Repeat with remaining beef and cream cheese mixture. Refrigerate for at least 1 hour or until firm. Cut into 1-in. slices. Serve on crackers. **Yield:** about 3 dozen.

TOMATO SHRIMP APPETIZER
Marguerite Martin, Southwest Harbor, Maine

I was given this delicious and festive recipe back when my husband was serving in the U.S. Coast Guard. It's been a huge hit at every party I've ever taken it to.

- 1 can (10-3/4 ounces) condensed tomato soup, undiluted
- 3 packages (3 ounces *each*) cream cheese, cubed
- 2 envelopes unflavored gelatin
- 1/4 cup cold water
- 3 cans (6 ounces *each*) small shrimp, rinsed and drained
- 1 cup mayonnaise
- 1 cup finely chopped celery
- 1 cup finely chopped green onions
- Assorted crackers

In a large saucepan, bring soup to a boil over medium heat, stirring frequently. Add cream cheese; cook and stir until smooth. Remove from the heat. In a small bowl, sprinkle gelatin over cold water; let stand for 1 minute. Stir into soup mixture until dissolved. Cool to room temperature.

Stir in the shrimp, mayonnaise, celery and onions. Refrigerate until slightly thickened, about 30 minutes. Pour into a 6-cup ring mold coated with nonstick spray. Chill until firm, about 4 hours. Unmold onto a serving platter; serve with crackers. **Yield:** 6 cups.

CREAM CHEESE FRUIT DIP
Sheryl Renner, El Paso, Texas

Color it Christmas with a platter of red and green apple slices piled 'round a bowl of this yummy no-fuss fruit dip! The dip also goes well with strawberries, grapes and kiwi.

- 1 package (8 ounces) cream cheese, softened
- 3/4 cup packed brown sugar
- 1 teaspoon vanilla extract
- Assorted fresh fruit

In a mixing bowl, combine the cream cheese, brown sugar and vanilla; mix well. Serve with fruit for dipping. Refrigerate leftovers. **Yield:** 1 cup.

Christmas Dinner

A FEAST FOR THE EYES. Happy holiday recipes include (clockwise from lower right) Orange-Pecan Pork Roast (p. 36), Banana Ice Cream Puffs (p. 36), Chicken Corn Bread Dressing (p. 36), Mushroom Spinach Salad (p. 37) and Honey-Glazed Carrots (p. 36).

Serve up hearty helpings of hospitality and good cheer when you prepare any of these festive recipes for your family's Christmas dinner!

ORANGE-PECAN PORK ROAST

Yvonne Novak, Silver Spring, Maryland
(Pictured on page 35)

Family and friends will "ooh" and "aah" when you bring in this impressive roast with its beautiful orange glaze and nutty topping. Moist and delicious, it's a real showstopper!

　　1 whole boneless pork loin roast (2-1/2 to 3 pounds)
1/2 cup finely chopped onion
　　1 garlic clove, minced
　　2 tablespoons vegetable oil
1/2 cup orange marmalade
1/4 cup chopped pecans
1/4 teaspoon ground cinnamon

Place roast on a rack in a shallow roasting pan. In a skillet, saute onion and garlic in oil until tender. Add the marmalade, pecans and cinnamon; cook and stir until marmalade is melted. Spoon over roast.
　　Bake, uncovered, at 325° for 1-3/4 hours or until a meat thermometer reads 160°. Let stand for 10 minutes before slicing. **Yield:** 6-8 servings.

CHICKEN CORN BREAD DRESSING

Fay Miller, Denham Springs, Louisiana
(Pictured on page 34)

Even though Mom passed away years ago, her wonderful corn bread dressing lives on each year at Christmas dinner. It just wouldn't be the same holiday without it!

　　1 broiler/fryer chicken (3 to 3-1/2 pounds)
2-1/2 quarts water
　　2 to 3 celery ribs with leaves
　　1 large onion, cut into chunks
DRESSING:
　　4 celery ribs, chopped
　　2 small onions, chopped
1/2 cup butter
　　1 teaspoon salt
1/4 teaspoon rubbed sage
1/4 teaspoon pepper
1/8 teaspoon cayenne pepper
　　6 cups crumbled corn bread
　　1 cup chopped green onions
3/4 cup chopped pecans, toasted
1/2 cup minced fresh parsley
　　2 eggs, lightly beaten

Place chicken in a soup kettle or Dutch oven. Add the water, celery and onion; bring to a boil. Reduce heat; cover and simmer for 1 to 1-1/2 hours or until chicken is tender. Remove chicken from broth. Strain broth, discarding vegetables; set broth aside. When cool enough to handle, remove chicken from bones; dice and place in a large bowl.
　　In a skillet, saute celery and onions in butter until tender; stir in the salt, sage, pepper and cayenne. Add to chicken. Stir in the corn bread, green onions, pecans, parsley and

eggs. Add 1-1/4 to 1-1/2 cups of reserved broth, stirring gently to mix. (Refrigerate remaining broth for another use.)
　　Transfer to a greased 13-in. x 9-in. x 2-in. baking dish. Cover and bake at 325° for 45 minutes. Uncover; bake 15-20 minutes longer or until a thermometer reads 160°. **Yield:** 12 servings.

HONEY-GLAZED CARROTS

Pat Gardetta, Osage Beach, Missouri
(Pictured on page 35)

These beautifully glazed carrots are colorful and dressed up enough for Christmas dinner. They have become such a favorite side dish that I often double the easy one-skillet recipe!

　　2 pounds baby carrots
1/4 cup finely chopped green onions
1/4 cup butter
1/4 cup honey
　　1 teaspoon grated orange peel
1/2 teaspoon salt
1/2 teaspoon ground cinnamon
1/4 teaspoon pepper
　　2 teaspoons cornstarch
1/2 cup orange juice
　　4 teaspoons minced fresh mint *or* minced fresh parsley

Place 1 in. of water in a skillet; add carrots. Bring to a boil. Reduce heat; cover and simmer for 15-20 minutes or until crisp-tender. Drain and set aside.
　　In the same skillet, saute green onions in butter until tender. Stir in the honey, orange peel, salt, cinnamon and pepper. Combine cornstarch and orange juice until smooth; stir into onion mixture. Bring to a boil; cook and stir for 1-2 minutes or until thickened.
　　Return carrots to the pan. Cook and stir for 2 minutes or until heated through. Sprinkle with mint. **Yield:** 8 servings.

BANANA ICE CREAM PUFFS

Pam Olson, Holland, Michigan
(Pictured on page 34)

These tender golden puffs are filled with rich banana ice cream and drizzled with hot fudge—making them pretty enough to draw a sleighful of compliments!

　　1 cup sugar
　　1 package (3.4 ounces) cook-and-serve banana cream pudding mix
　　3 tablespoons all-purpose flour
1/2 teaspoon salt
　　5 cups milk
　　4 eggs, lightly beaten
　　4 cups heavy whipping cream
1-3/4 cups mashed ripe bananas (about 4 medium)
　　2 tablespoons vanilla extract

CREAM PUFFS:
>   2 cups water
>   1 cup butter
>   2 teaspoons sugar
> 1/4 teaspoon salt
>   2 cups all-purpose flour
>   8 eggs
> Hot fudge *or* chocolate ice cream topping
> Chopped nuts

In a saucepan, combine the sugar, pudding mix, flour and salt; gradually stir in milk until smooth. Cook and stir over medium heat until thickened and bubbly. Reduce heat; cook and stir 2 minutes longer. Remove from the heat.

Stir a small amount of hot filling into eggs. Return all to the pan, stirring constantly. Bring to a gentle boil; cook and stir for 2 minutes. Press plastic wrap onto the surface of pudding mixture. Refrigerate until chilled, about 4 hours.

Stir in the cream, bananas and vanilla. Fill cylinder of ice cream freezer two-thirds full; freeze according to manufacturer's directions. Refrigerate remaining mixture until ready to freeze. Allow ice cream to ripen in the refrigerator freezer for 2-4 hours.

In a large saucepan, bring the water, butter, sugar and salt to a boil. Add flour all at once and stir until a smooth ball forms. Remove from the heat; let stand for 5 minutes. Add eggs, two at a time, beating well after each addition. Continue beating until mixture is smooth and shiny.

Drop by 2 rounded tablespoonfuls 3 in. apart onto greased baking sheets. Bake at 400° for 20-25 minutes or until golden brown. Remove to wire racks. Immediately split puffs open; remove tops and set aside. Discard soft dough from inside. Cool puffs.

To serve, spoon banana ice cream into cream puffs; replace tops. Drizzle with hot fudge topping and sprinkle with nuts. **Yield:** about 2 dozen puffs and 3 quarts ice cream.

MUSHROOM SPINACH SALAD
Melissa Ward, Yucaipa, California
(Pictured on page 35)

I found this recipe in our newspaper and couldn't wait to try it. The tangy hint of barbecue sauce in the dressing makes it a big hit with my family.

>   1 package (6 ounces) fresh baby spinach
>   4 ounces fresh mushrooms, sliced
>   1 can (8 ounces) sliced water chestnuts, drained
>   2 hard-cooked eggs, coarsely chopped
> 1/4 cup thinly sliced green onions
>   2 bacon strips, cooked and crumbled
> **DRESSING:**
> 1/3 cup olive oil
>   3 tablespoons barbecue sauce
>   2 tablespoons sugar
>   2 tablespoons cider vinegar
>   1 tablespoon Worcestershire sauce
> 1/8 teaspoon garlic powder
> 1/8 teaspoon onion salt
> 1/8 teaspoon pepper

In a large salad bowl, toss the spinach, mushrooms, water chestnuts, eggs, onions and bacon. In a jar with a tight-fitting lid, combine the dressing ingredients; shake well.

Drizzle over the salad; toss to coat. Serve immediately. **Yield:** 8-10 servings.

STUFFED FLANK STEAK
Bernice McFadden, Dayton, Ohio
(Pictured below)

This is one of my family's favorite beef recipes. Tasty, tender and tucked full of vegetables, it warms us up often on cold winter nights.

>   1 beef flank steak (about 1-1/4 pounds)
> 1/2 cup soy sauce
> 1/4 cup vegetable oil
>   2 tablespoons molasses
>   2 teaspoons ground mustard
>   1 teaspoon ground ginger
>   1 garlic clove, minced
> 1-1/2 cups cooked long grain rice
>   1 medium carrot, shredded
> 1/2 cup sliced water chestnuts
> 1/4 cup sliced green onions

Starting along one long side, cut a horizontal slit through the steak to within 1/2 in. of the opposite side. Place in a greased 13-in. x 9-in. x 2-in. baking dish. Combine the soy sauce, oil, molasses, mustard, ginger and garlic; set aside 1/4 cup. Pour remaining marinade over meat. Let stand for 30 minutes.

Meanwhile, combine the rice, carrot, water chestnuts, onions and reserved marinade. Stuff into steak. Cover and bake at 350° for 45 minutes. Uncover; baste with pan drippings. Bake 15-20 minutes longer or until meat is tender. Brush again with pan drippings if desired. **Yield:** 4 servings.

CRAB TARTLETS
Janice Wolters, Edmonton, Alberta

Every time I serve these tiny tasty tarts, I'm asked for the recipe. Holiday guests of all ages simply gobble them up! I've found that finely chopped leftover ham makes a handy substitute for the crab.

    3 packages (2.1 ounces *each*) miniature phyllo tart shells
1/2 cup shredded Swiss cheese
    2 eggs
1/3 cup mayonnaise
1/4 cup half-and-half cream
    1 green onion, finely chopped
1/4 teaspoon salt
1/4 teaspoon ground mustard
1/8 teaspoon pepper
    1 can (6 ounces) crabmeat, drained, flaked and cartilage removed

Place tart shells on an ungreased baking sheet. Sprinkle Swiss cheese into each shell. In a mixing bowl, combine the remaining ingredients. Spoon a teaspoonful of crab mixture into each tart shell. Bake at 375° for 18-20 minutes or until pastry is browned. Serve warm. **Yield:** 45 tartlets.

CHOCOLATE MACAROON CAKE
Madeline Prom, Port Washington, Wisconsin

As youngsters, my 10 children always loved this moist fudgy cake with the coconut center. It's still at the top of their request list when my crowd of 46 comes home for the holidays!

    1 egg white
    2 teaspoons vanilla extract, *divided*
2-1/4 cups sugar, *divided*
    2 cups flaked coconut
1/2 cup shortening
    3 eggs
    1 egg yolk
1/2 cup sour cream
    2 cups all-purpose flour
1/2 cup baking cocoa
    1 teaspoon baking soda
1/2 teaspoon salt
3/4 cup strong brewed coffee
CHOCOLATE CREAM FROSTING:
    3 tablespoons butter, softened
1-1/2 cups semisweet chocolate chips, melted
    2 cups confectioners' sugar
    7 to 8 tablespoons milk

In a small mixing bowl, beat the egg white and 1 teaspoon vanilla on medium speed until soft peaks form. Gradually beat in 1/2 cup sugar, about 2 tablespoons at a time, on high until glossy stiff peaks form. Fold in the coconut. Set aside.

In a large mixing bowl, cream shortening and remaining sugar. Beat in the eggs, egg yolk, sour cream and remaining vanilla until light and fluffy. Combine the flour, cocoa, baking soda and salt; add to creamed mixture alternately with coffee.

Pour half of the batter into a greased 10-in. tube pan with removable bottom. Top with coconut mixture; spread with the remaining batter. Bake at 350° for 55-60 minutes or until a toothpick inserted near the center comes out clean. Cool for 10 minutes before removing from pan to a wire rack to cool completely.

In a small mixing bowl, combine frosting ingredients; beat until smooth. Spread over the top and sides of cake. **Yield:** 12-16 servings.

ROSY-RED CHRISTMAS APPLES
Patsy Woods, Waycross, Georgia
(Pictured below)

Pretty enough to pass as dessert, these sweet festive apples make a nice alternative to salad. The creamy nut-filled mixture stuffed inside is delightful.

    2 cups sugar
    1 cup water
    1 teaspoon red liquid food coloring
  16 medium apples, peeled and cored
    1 package (8 ounces) cream cheese, softened
1/2 cup chopped pecans
    2 tablespoons mayonnaise

In a large saucepan, bring sugar, water and food coloring to a boil. Place four apples in pan; boil for 3 minutes. Turn apples over; boil 2-5 minutes longer or until apples are crisp-tender. Place in a large dish to cool. Repeat with remaining apples.

In a small bowl, combine the cream cheese, pecans and mayonnaise. Stuff into center of apples. Serve or refrigerate. **Yield:** 16 servings.

GERMAN RED CABBAGE
Ardis Stauffer, Ida Grove, Iowa

If your family likes the sweet-tart flavor found in many German dishes, they'll enjoy this recipe. The cabbage, apples and onions are cooked with vinegar, sugar and a variety of spices—the end result can't be beat!

    1 medium head red cabbage, cored and sliced
    2 large tart apples, peeled and sliced
    1 medium sweet onion, sliced and separated into
      rings
1-1/2 cups water
    1 cup cider vinegar
  1/2 cup sugar
    1 tablespoon butter
    1 teaspoon salt
    6 whole peppercorns
    2 whole allspice
    2 whole cloves
    1 bay leaf
    2 teaspoons cornstarch
    2 teaspoons cold water

In a Dutch oven, toss the cabbage, apples and onion. Add water, vinegar, sugar, butter and salt. Place the peppercorns, allspice, cloves and bay leaf on a double thickness of cheesecloth; bring up corners of cloth and tie with kitchen string to form a bag. Add to Dutch oven. Bring to a boil. Reduce heat; cover and simmer for 1-1/4 hours.

Discard spice bag. In a small bowl, combine cornstarch and cold water until smooth; stir into cabbage mixture. Bring to a boil; cook and stir for 1-2 minutes or until thickened. **Yield:** 6-8 servings.

STUFFED SHELLS WITH MEAT SAUCE
Sunny Folding, Blair, Nebraska

Even my "meat-and-potatoes" husband often requests these filling and flavorful shells. Chock-full of veggies and cheese, they make great cold-weather fare.

   28 jumbo pasta shells
    1 pound ground beef
  1/2 cup chopped onion
    1 garlic clove, minced
    1 can (29 ounces) tomato sauce
    1 can (28 ounces) Italian diced tomatoes, well
      drained
1-1/2 teaspoons dried oregano, *divided*
  1/2 teaspoon dried basil
    2 eggs, lightly beaten
    3 cups (24 ounces) small-curd cottage cheese
    2 packages (10 ounces *each*) frozen chopped
      spinach, thawed and squeezed dry
    2 cups (8 ounces) shredded mozzarella cheese
  1/2 cup grated Parmesan cheese
  1/2 teaspoon seasoned salt

Cook pasta shells according to package directions. Meanwhile, in a skillet, cook the beef, onion and garlic over medium heat until meat is no longer pink; drain. Stir in the tomato sauce, tomatoes, 1/2 teaspoon oregano and basil.

Bring to a boil. Reduce heat; simmer, uncovered, for 10-15 minutes.

In a large bowl, combine the eggs, cottage cheese, spinach, mozzarella cheese, Parmesan cheese, seasoned salt and remaining oregano. Drain pasta shells; cool slightly. Stuff with cheese mixture.

Spread 1 cup of meat sauce into each of two greased 11-in. x 7-in. x 2-in. baking dishes; arrange shells over sauce in a single layer. Pour remaining meat sauce over the shells. Cover and bake at 350° for 40-50 minutes or until a thermometer reads 160°. **Yield:** 6-8 servings.

GOLDEN CHEDDAR MUFFINS
Mae Keller, Aurora, Colorado

Since receiving this fuss-free recipe from a wonderful cook at work, I've made these savory muffins for many a holiday dinner and brunch. They are moist and tender and always a hit with my guests!

    2 cups all-purpose flour
4-1/2 teaspoons sugar
1-1/2 teaspoons baking powder
  1/2 teaspoon baking soda
  1/2 teaspoon salt
    1 egg, beaten
    1 cup buttermilk
  1/3 cup butter, melted
    2 teaspoons spicy brown mustard
  1/8 teaspoon hot pepper sauce
    1 cup (4 ounces) shredded cheddar cheese

In a large bowl, combine the first five ingredients. Combine the egg, buttermilk, butter, mustard and hot pepper sauce; stir into the dry ingredients just until moistened. Fold in the cheese.

Fill greased or paper-lined muffin cups two-thirds full. Bake at 400° for 15-20 minutes or until a toothpick inserted in muffin comes out clean. Cool for 5 minutes before removing from pan to a wire rack. Serve warm. Refrigerate any leftovers. **Yield:** 1 dozen.

CRANBERRY COLESLAW
Sammy Daken, Kelliher, Minnesota

I love trying new recipes, and my family enjoys most of my "experiments". Salads are always in demand at our house, and this one is fast, festive and refreshing.

  1/2 cup mayonnaise
    1 to 2 tablespoons honey
    1 teaspoon cider vinegar
  1/2 teaspoon salt
  1/4 teaspoon celery seed
Dash pepper
    3 cups shredded cabbage
  1/4 cup chopped fresh *or* frozen cranberries

In a small bowl, combine the first six ingredients. Place cabbage in a serving bowl. Add mayonnaise mixture and toss to coat evenly. Fold in cranberries. Serve immediately. **Yield:** 4 servings.

Cookie Creations

CHRISTMAS TREATS to bake by the dozen include (clockwise from lower right) Poinsettia Cookies (p. 42), Yuletide Cherry Cookies (p. 42), Lime Christmas Tree Cookies (p. 43), Apricot Tea Cookies (p. 42) and elegant Raspberry Sandwich Spritz (p. 42).

Bring back merry mouth-watering memories with batches of old-fashioned bars and home-baked Christmas cookies trimmed in delicious holiday style.

POINSETTIA COOKIES
Patricia Eckard, Harrisonburg, Virginia
(Pictured on page 41)

I must make 30 different kinds of cookies during the Christmas season—many to give away as gifts. Judging from the comments I get, these pretty pink poinsettias with a hint of cinnamon flavor are not just my own personal favorite!

    1 cup butter, softened
    1 cup confectioners' sugar
    1 egg
    2 to 3 drops red food coloring
2-1/3 cups all-purpose flour
    3/4 teaspoon salt
    1/4 cup finely crushed red-hot candies
FROSTING:
    1 cup confectioners' sugar
    4 teaspoons milk
Additional red-hot candies

In a large mixing bowl, cream butter and confectioners' sugar. Beat in egg and food coloring. Combine flour and salt; gradually add to the creamed mixture. Stir in red-hots. Divide dough in half; wrap in plastic wrap. Refrigerate for at least 1 hour or until firm.

On a lightly floured surface, roll out one portion of dough into a 12-in. x 10-in. rectangle. With a sharp knife or pastry wheel, cut dough into 2-in. squares. Place 1 in. apart on lightly greased baking sheets. Cut through dough from each corner of square to within 1/2 in. of center. Fold alternating points of square to center to form a pinwheel; pinch gently at center to seal. Repeat with remaining dough.

Bake at 350° for 7-9 minutes or until set. Remove to wire racks to cool. Combine the confectioners' sugar and milk. Pipe 1/2 teaspoon frosting in the center of each cookie; top with a red-hot. **Yield:** 5 dozen.

RASPBERRY SANDWICH SPRITZ
Joan O'Brien, Punta Gorda, Florida
(Pictured on page 41)

I started baking these Christmas classics when I was a sophomore in high school…and I am still making them now for my grown children and grandkids. The combination of jam, buttery shortbread, chocolate and sprinkles adds up to a fancy and festive treat.

    1 cup butter, softened
   3/4 cup sugar
    1 egg
    1 teaspoon vanilla extract
2-1/4 cups all-purpose flour
    1/2 teaspoon salt
    1/4 teaspoon baking powder
    1 cup seedless raspberry jam
    1 cup (6 ounces) semisweet chocolate chips
Chocolate sprinkles

In a large mixing bowl, cream butter and sugar. Beat in egg and vanilla. Combine the flour, salt and baking powder; gradually add to creamed mixture.

Using a cookie press fitted with a ribbon disk, form dough into long strips on ungreased baking sheets. Cut each strip into 2-in. pieces (do not separate). Bake at 375° for 8-10 minutes or until edges are golden brown. Cut again if necessary. Remove to wire racks to cool.

Spread the bottom of half of the cookies with jam; top with remaining cookies. In a microwave, melt chocolate chips; stir until smooth. Place chocolate sprinkles in a bowl. Dip each end of cookies in melted chocolate, then in sprinkles. Place on waxed paper; let stand until firm. **Yield:** about 4-1/2 dozen.

YULETIDE CHERRY COOKIES
Verna Hofer, Mitchell, South Dakota
(Pictured on page 40)

Crispy on the outside, these eye-catching cherry-topped cookies are chewy and tender on the inside. They're a great hit whenever I take them to holiday parties or cookie exchanges!

    1/2 cup butter, softened
    1 package (3 ounces) cream cheese, softened
    1/2 cup sugar
    1/4 teaspoon almond extract
    1 cup all-purpose flour
    1 teaspoon baking powder
    1/8 teaspoon salt
    3/4 cup crushed crisp rice cereal
   15 red *and/or* green maraschino cherries, halved
      and patted dry

In a large mixing bowl, cream the butter, cream cheese and sugar. Beat in almond extract. Combine the flour, baking powder and salt; gradually add to the creamed mixture. Cover and refrigerate for 1 hour or until easy to handle.

Shape dough into 1-in. balls; roll in crushed cereal. Place 2 in. apart on ungreased baking sheets. Bake at 350° for 12-15 minutes or until lightly browned. Immediately press a cherry half into the center of each cookie. Remove to wire racks to cool. **Yield:** 2-1/2 dozen.

APRICOT TEA COOKIES
Judith McVickers, Pittsburg, Kansas
(Pictured on page 40)

It just wouldn't be Christmas without these dainty melt-in-the-mouth cookies on my platter! Filled with apricots and drizzled with frosty glaze, they couldn't be more delectable.

1-1/4 cups all-purpose flour
    6 tablespoons sugar
    1/8 teaspoon salt
    4 ounces cream cheese

    1/2 cup cold butter
      1 tablespoon sour cream
FILLING:
1-1/4 cups chopped dried apricots
  1/2 cup sugar
    5 tablespoons orange juice
GLAZE:
    1 cup confectioners' sugar
    4 teaspoons water

In a large mixing bowl, combine the flour, sugar and salt. Cut in the cream cheese and butter until mixture resembles coarse crumbs. Add sour cream, tossing with a fork until dough forms a ball. Cover and refrigerate for at least 1 hour.

Meanwhile, combine filling ingredients in a saucepan; bring to a boil. Reduce heat; cover and simmer for 10 minutes. Uncover; simmer 7-9 minutes longer or until most of the liquid is absorbed, stirring occasionally. Set the filling aside to cool.

Divide dough in half. On a well-floured surface, roll out each portion into a 10-in. square; cut each into 2-in. squares. Place about 1/2 teaspoon of filling in the center of each square. Bring two opposite corners of square to the center; pinch firmly to seal. Place on greased baking sheets. Bake at 325° for 18-20 minutes or until edges are lightly browned. Remove to wire racks to cool. Combine the glaze ingredients; drizzle over cooled cookies. **Yield:** about 4 dozen.

LIME CHRISTMAS TREE COOKIES
Mary Ann Taday, East Lyme, Connecticut
(Pictured on page 40)

Luscious with lime juice and flecked with pistachio nuts, these tangy frosted fir trees are almost too pretty to eat! They're a delightful addition to Yuletide cookie trays.

      1 cup butter, softened
  1/2 cup sugar
  1/4 cup lime juice
      2 teaspoons grated lime peel
      1 teaspoon vanilla extract
2-3/4 cups all-purpose flour
    10 to 12 drops green food coloring
  3/4 cup finely chopped pistachios
FROSTING:
      1 package (3 ounces) cream cheese, softened
      1 cup confectioners' sugar
      1 teaspoon lime juice
Green colored sugar

In a large mixing bowl, cream butter and sugar. Beat in lime juice, lime peel and vanilla. Gradually add flour. Beat in food coloring. Stir in pistachios. Cover and refrigerate for 4 hours or until easy to handle.

On a lightly floured surface, roll out dough to 1/4-in. thickness. Cut with a floured 2-1/2-in. tree-shaped cookie cutter. Place 1 in. apart on ungreased baking sheets. Bake at 350° for 8-10 minutes or until set. Cool for 5 minutes before removing from pans to wire racks to cool completely.

In a small mixing bowl, beat the cream cheese, confectioners' sugar and lime juice until smooth. Decorate cookies with frosting as desired and sprinkle with colored sugar. Store in the refrigerator. **Yield:** about 4 dozen.

FUDGY CHERRY BROWNIES
Jeanne Hartman, Littlestown, Pennsylvania
(Pictured below)

When I first saw this recipe in a local newspaper years ago, I couldn't wait to try it for our guests that very night. I knew it was a winner from the first bite. These rich fudgy brownies have been making friends merry ever since!

      2 cups (12 ounces) semisweet chocolate chips,
        divided
  1/4 cup butter, softened
      2 cups biscuit/baking mix
      1 can (14 ounces) sweetened condensed milk
      1 egg
  1/2 teaspoon almond extract
  1/2 cup chopped maraschino cherries
  1/3 cup sliced almonds, toasted

In a heavy saucepan or microwave, melt 1 cup chocolate chips and butter; stir until smooth. In a mixing bowl, combine biscuit mix, milk, egg and almond extract. Stir in chocolate mixture; mix well. Fold in cherries and remaining chocolate chips.

Pour into a greased 13-in. x 9-in. x 2-in. baking pan. Sprinkle with almonds. Bake at 350° for 20-25 minutes or until a toothpick inserted near the center comes out with moist crumbs and the edges pull away from sides. Cool on a wire rack. **Yield:** 3 dozen.

HOLIDAY MINIATURES
Elaine Million, Denver, Indiana
(Pictured above)

White candy coating adds sweetness to these bite-size treats. Adding sprinkles and colored sugar to my mom's recipe makes them as much fun to bake as to eat.

    1 cup butter, softened
1/4 cup sugar
    1 teaspoon vanilla extract
    1 teaspoon lemon juice
    2 cups plus 2 tablespoons all-purpose flour
    1 pound white candy coating
Colored sugar *and/or* nonpareils

In a large mixing bowl, cream butter and sugar. Beat in vanilla and lemon juice. Gradually add flour. Divide dough in half. Wrap in plastic wrap; refrigerate for 30 minutes or until easy to handle.

On a lightly floured surface, roll out each portion of dough to 1/4-in. thickness. Cut with floured 1-in. cookie cutters. Place 1 in. apart on ungreased baking sheets. Bake at 350° for 10-12 minutes or until lightly browned. Remove to wire racks to cool.

In a microwave, melt candy coating. Dip cookies in coating and place on waxed paper-lined baking sheets. Sprinkle with colored sugar and/or nonpareils. Refrigerate for 30 minutes or until set. **Yield:** 10 dozen.

MINCEMEAT COOKIES
Betty Jorsvick, Olds, Alberta

You can taste the spirit of Christmases past in these chewy old-fashioned cookies with their sweet caramel frosting. One batch makes 9 dozen cookies that freeze well for the holidays!

    1 cup butter, softened
1-1/2 cups sugar
    3 eggs
3-1/4 cups prepared mincemeat
3-3/4 cups all-purpose flour
    1 teaspoon baking powder
    1 teaspoon baking soda
    1 teaspoon ground cinnamon
1/4 teaspoon salt
    1 cup chopped pecans
FROSTING:
1-1/2 cups packed brown sugar
    3/4 cup butter, cubed
    1 cup confectioners' sugar
    6 tablespoons half-and-half cream
    1 teaspoon rum extract
    9 dozen pecan halves

In a large mixing bowl, cream butter and sugar. Beat in the eggs. Add mincemeat; mix well. Combine the flour, baking powder, baking soda, cinnamon and salt; add to the creamed mixture and mix well. Stir in pecans. Drop by rounded tablespoonfuls 2 in. apart onto greased baking sheets. Bake at 350° for 14-16 minutes or until edges begin to brown. Remove to wire racks to cool.

For the frosting, combine the brown sugar and butter in a saucepan; bring to a boil over medium heat. Boil for 6-8 minutes, stirring twice, or until the sugar is dissolved. Remove from the heat. Add the confectioners' sugar, cream and extract; beat until smooth. Frost the cookies; top each with a pecan half. **Yield:** 9 dozen.

TRIPLE-LAYER MOCHA BARS
Marjorie Van Riper, Ralston, Nebraska

Layered with flavors of malted milk, coffee and coconut, these rich blue-ribbon bars win rave reviews every holiday season.

1-3/4 cups all-purpose flour
    2/3 cup packed brown sugar
    3/4 cup cold butter
FILLING:
    3 eggs
1/2 cup sugar
    2 teaspoons vanilla extract
    3/4 cup chocolate malted milk powder
1/4 cup all-purpose flour
    1 teaspoon baking soda
1/4 teaspoon salt
    1 cup flaked coconut
1/2 cup chopped walnuts
FROSTING:
1-1/2 cups confectioners' sugar
    3 tablespoons chocolate malted milk powder
    2 tablespoons strong brewed coffee
    2 tablespoons butter, melted
    1 teaspoon vanilla extract

In a bowl, combine the flour and brown sugar; cut in butter until crumbly. Press into a greased 13-in. x 9-in. x 2-in. baking pan. Bake at 350° for 8-10 minutes or until golden brown.

In a mixing bowl, beat eggs until foamy. Add the sugar and vanilla; mix well. Combine the malted milk powder, flour, baking soda and salt; add to egg mixture. Fold in the coconut and walnuts. Spread over prepared crust. Bake for 25-30 minutes or until a toothpick inserted near the center comes out clean. Cool on a wire rack.

In a mixing bowl, combine the frosting ingredients. Spread over cooled bars. Store in the refrigerator. **Yield:** about 3 dozen.

FROSTED PECAN BUTTER COOKIES
Myrl Solum, Rudyard, Montana

Lemon frosting gives my delicate cream-colored butter cookies a special zest. The citrusy hint of sunshine is extra welcome in winter, and crispy pecans fill every delicious bite.

    1 cup butter, softened
    3/4 cup confectioners' sugar
    2 tablespoons milk
1-1/2 cups all-purpose flour
    3/4 cup cornstarch
    1/2 cup finely chopped pecans
LEMON FROSTING:
2-1/2 cups confectioners' sugar
    3 tablespoons lemon juice
    1 tablespoon butter, melted
    1 to 2 drops yellow food coloring, optional

In a large mixing bowl, cream butter and confectioners' sugar; beat in milk. Combine flour and cornstarch; gradually add to creamed mixture. Cover and refrigerate for 1 hour or until easy to handle.

Roll dough into 1-in. balls. Dip each ball halfway into pecans. Place nut side down 2 in. apart on ungreased baking sheets. Flatten slightly. Bake at 350° for 13-15 minutes or until lightly browned. Remove to wire racks to cool. In a small bowl, combine frosting ingredients until smooth. Frost cooled cookies. **Yield:** 4 dozen.

CHOCOLATE-DIPPED COCONUT SNOWBALLS
Emily Barrett, Wyoming, Pennsylvania

If you like the taste of coconut and chocolate, you can't help but love these fancy and festive-looking cookies.

    1/3 cup butter, softened
    2/3 cup packed brown sugar
      1 egg
    1/2 teaspoon vanilla extract
1-1/3 cups all-purpose flour
    1/4 teaspoon baking powder
    1/4 teaspoon baking soda
    1/4 teaspoon salt
      1 package (4 ounces) German sweet chocolate, finely chopped
    1/2 cup flaked coconut
    1/2 cup finely chopped pecans, toasted
TOPPING:
    12 squares (1 ounce *each*) semisweet chocolate
      4 teaspoons shortening
2-1/2 cups flaked coconut, toasted

In a large mixing bowl, cream butter and brown sugar. Beat in egg and vanilla. Combine the flour, baking powder, baking soda and salt; gradually add to creamed mixture and mix well. Stir in the German sweet chocolate, coconut and pecans. Roll into 3/4-in. balls. Place 2 in. apart on ungreased baking sheets. Bake at 350° for 10-12 minutes or until edges are browned. Remove to wire racks to cool.

Break each square of semisweet chocolate into four pieces. In a microwave, melt chocolate and shortening; stir until smooth. Dip cookies halfway into chocolate; allow excess

to drip off. Place on waxed paper-lined baking sheets; sprinkle with toasted coconut. Chill for 1 hour or until firm. **Yield:** about 5-1/2 dozen.

CRANBERRY WALNUT COOKIES
Joyce Larson, Kiester, Minnesota

When I brought these cookies in for the holiday open house at work, they simply disappeared—150 dozen of them!

      1 cup butter-flavored shortening
      1 cup sugar
    2/3 cup packed brown sugar
      2 eggs
      1 tablespoon orange juice concentrate
      1 tablespoon grated orange peel
      2 teaspoons vanilla extract
2-1/2 cups all-purpose flour
      1 teaspoon cream of tartar
      1 teaspoon baking soda
      1 teaspoon salt
      1 cup coarsely chopped fresh cranberries
      1 cup chopped walnuts

In a large mixing bowl, cream shortening and sugars. Beat in eggs, one at a time. Add orange juice concentrate, orange peel and vanilla. Combine the flour, cream of tartar, baking soda and salt; gradually add to creamed mixture and mix well. Stir in cranberries and walnuts. Cover and refrigerate for 2 hours or until easy to handle.

Drop by tablespoonfuls onto greased baking sheets. Bake at 350° for 14-16 minutes or until lightly browned. Remove to wire racks to cool. **Yield:** 4 dozen.

DIPPED MACAROONS
Lillian McDivitt, Rochester Hills, Michigan

I always get compliments from my kids, grandkids and great-grandkids on these elegant cookies. Dipping macaroons in raspberry-flavored chocolate makes them uncommonly good!

2-2/3 cups flaked coconut
    2/3 cup sugar
      6 tablespoons all-purpose flour
    1/4 teaspoon salt
      4 egg whites
    1/2 to 1 teaspoon almond extract
      2 cups raspberry chips*
      1 tablespoon shortening

In a large mixing bowl, combine the coconut, sugar, flour and salt. Stir in egg whites and almond extract; mix well. Drop by rounded teaspoonfuls onto greased baking sheets. Bake at 325° for 15-20 minutes or until golden brown. Cool for 2 minutes before removing to wire racks.

In a microwave-safe bowl, combine raspberry chips and shortening. Cover and microwave on high for 1-2 minutes or until chips are melted; stir until smooth. Dip half of each cookie in mixture; allow excess to drip off. Place on waxed paper; let stand until set. **Yield:** about 3 dozen.

*Editor's Note: This recipe was tested with Hershey's raspberry chips with semisweet chocolate.

Dazzling Desserts

*Top off gala Yuletide meals with a finale that echoes the joyful strains of the season!
Guests will delight over a medley of these irresistible desserts and tempting sweets.*

SOUTHERN CHOCOLATE TORTE
Ginger George Gentry, Sutherlin, Virginia
(Pictured on page 46)

This towering torte takes guests' breath away every time! It's my most-requested cake recipe, has an unforgettable frosting and makes a grand showpiece for any holiday spread.

- 1 package (18-1/4 ounces) Swiss chocolate *or* devil's food cake mix
- 1 package (3.4 ounces) instant vanilla pudding mix
- 3 eggs
- 1-1/4 cups milk
- 1/2 cup vegetable oil

FROSTING:
- 1 package (8 ounces) cream cheese, softened
- 1 cup sugar
- 1 cup confectioners' sugar
- 10 milk chocolate candy bars with almonds (1.45 ounces *each*), *divided*
- 1 carton (16 ounces) frozen whipped topping, *thawed*

In a large mixing bowl, sift together the cake and pudding mixes. In another bowl, whisk the eggs, milk and oil. Add to dry ingredients; beat until well blended. Pour into three greased and floured 9-in. round baking pans. Bake at 350° for 20-25 minutes or until a toothpick inserted near the center comes out clean. Cool for 10 minutes before removing from pans to wire racks to cool completely.

In a small mixing bowl, beat the cream cheese and sugars until smooth. Finely chop eight candy bars; stir into cream cheese mixture. Fold in whipped topping. Spread frosting on cake plate, between layers and over the top and sides of the cake. Chop the remaining candy bars; sprinkle over top and along bottom edge of cake. Refrigerate overnight in an airtight container. **Yield:** 12 servings.

CHERRY BERRY CHEESECAKE
Susan Knittle-Hunter, Evanston, Wyoming
(Pictured on page 46)

I found this merry prize-winning recipe in a magazine years ago. It's been a Yuletide tradition at our house ever since.

2-1/4 cups sliced almonds, toasted
1/4 cup confectioners' sugar
1 teaspoon grated orange peel
3/4 teaspoon ground cinnamon
1/4 teaspoon ground nutmeg
1/4 cup butter, melted
FRUIT FILLING:
1 can (21 ounces) cherry pie filling

DECK YOUR TABLE with such delectable desserts as scrumptious Southern Chocolate Torte, Frozen Raspberry Delight and Cherry Berry Cheesecake (p. 46, clockwise from top).

---

1 cup whole-berry cranberry sauce
3 tablespoons sugar
1 teaspoon lemon juice
1 envelope unflavored gelatin
CREAM CHEESE FILLING:
2 packages (3 ounces *each*) cream cheese, softened
3 tablespoons confectioners' sugar
2 tablespoons plain yogurt
Additional sliced almonds

Place almonds in a food processor or blender; cover and process until finely ground. Transfer to a bowl; add the confectioners' sugar, orange peel, cinnamon and nutmeg. Stir in butter. Press onto the bottom and 1 in. up the sides of a greased 9-in. springform pan. Bake at 350° for 9-11 minutes or until lightly browned; cool.

In a saucepan, combine the pie filling, cranberry sauce, sugar and lemon juice. Sprinkle gelatin over cranberry mixture. Stir until combined; let stand for 1 minute. Cook over low heat until gelatin is completely dissolved, stirring gently. Remove from the heat. Chill until slightly thickened.

Meanwhile, in a mixing bowl, beat the cream cheese, confectioners' sugar and yogurt until smooth. Spread evenly over cooled crust. Spoon fruit filling over the cream cheese layer. Refrigerate for at least 6 hours or overnight. Sprinkle with sliced almonds. Refrigerate any leftovers. **Yield:** 12 servings.

FROZEN RASPBERRY DELIGHT
Nora Schuffenhauer, River Edge, New Jersey
(Pictured on page 46)

Light and refreshing, here's a dessert created with busy holiday hostesses in mind. It's easy, lovely, serves a crowd and can be made days ahead for convenience.

2 cups chocolate wafer crumbs (about 32 cookies)
1/3 cup butter, melted
1/4 cup sugar
1 cup hot fudge ice cream topping, warmed
2 quarts vanilla ice cream or frozen vanilla yogurt, slightly softened
2 pints raspberry sherbet
1 carton (8 ounces) frozen whipped topping, thawed
Mint leaves and fresh raspberries, optional

In a bowl, combine cookie crumbs, butter and sugar. Press into an ungreased 13-in. x 9-in. x 2-in. dish. Refrigerate for 15 minutes. Carefully spread hot fudge topping over the crust. Spoon ice cream over topping; spread evenly. Spread raspberry sherbet over ice cream; swirl gently. Top with whipped topping. Cover and freeze for 8 hours or overnight.

Remove from the freezer 10-15 minutes before serving. Garnish with mint and raspberries if desired. Cut into squares. **Yield:** 12-15 servings.

FUDGE-FILLED DESSERT STRIPS
Kimberly Santoro, Stuart, Florida

This family favorite was handed down to me by my mother, and everyone who tastes the flaky chocolate-filled strips asks for the recipe. They're delicious!

>   1 cup butter, softened
>   1 package (8 ounces) cream cheese, softened
>   2 cups all-purpose flour
>   2 cups (12 ounces) semisweet chocolate chips
>   1 can (14 ounces) sweetened condensed milk
>   2 cups chopped walnuts
> Confectioners' sugar, optional

In a large mixing bowl, cream butter and cream cheese. Gradually add the flour. Turn onto a lightly floured surface; knead until smooth, about 3 minutes. Divide dough into fourths; cover and refrigerate for 1-2 hours or until easy to handle.

In a heavy saucepan, melt the chocolate chips and milk. Stir in the walnuts. Cool to room temperature. Roll out each portion of dough onto an ungreased baking sheet into an 11-in. x 6-1/2-in. rectangle. Spread 3/4 cup chocolate filling down the center of each rectangle. Fold long sides to the center; press to seal all edges. Turn over so seam side is down.

Bake at 350° for 27-32 minutes or until lightly browned. Remove to wire racks to cool. Cut into 1/2-in. slices. Dust with confectioners' sugar if desired. **Yield:** 3 dozen.

STRAWBERRY RICE DESSERT
Judy Benson, Granite Falls, Minnesota

A snowy wreath of creamy rice pudding crowned with a pretty red strawberry filling makes this dessert a colorful Christmas classic. It's also nice layered in parfait glasses and garnished with green mint leaves.

>   1/2 cup uncooked long grain rice
> 1-3/4 cups cold milk, *divided*
>   1/2 teaspoon salt
>   1 package unflavored gelatin
>   1/2 cup sugar
>   1 cup heavy whipping cream, whipped
> FILLING:
>   2 packages (10 ounces *each*) frozen sweetened
>   sliced strawberries, thawed
>   2 tablespoons cornstarch
>   1 tablespoon lemon juice

In a saucepan, combine the rice, 1-1/2 cups milk and salt. Bring to a boil over medium heat, stirring frequently. Reduce heat; cover and simmer for 20 minutes or until liquid is absorbed and rice is tender.

In a microwave-safe bowl, sprinkle gelatin over remaining milk; let stand for 1 minute. Stir in sugar. Microwave on high for 45 seconds; stir. Let stand for 1 minute or until gelatin and sugar are completely dissolved. Stir into hot rice. Transfer to a bowl. Refrigerate until chilled, about 1 hour. Fold in the whipped cream. Spoon into a 5-cup ring mold coated with nonstick cooking spray. Refrigerate for at least 2 hours or until firm.

Meanwhile, drain the strawberries, reserving 1 cup juice.

In a saucepan, combine cornstarch and reserved strawberry juice until smooth. Bring to a boil; cook and stir for 2 minutes or until thickened. Remove from the heat; stir in lemon juice. Cool for 10 minutes. Add strawberries and stir to coat. Refrigerate until chilled. Invert rice mold onto a serving platter and unmold. Fill center with strawberry mixture. Garnish with mint if desired. **Yield:** 6 servings.

CHOCOLATE DESSERT DELIGHT
Lee Ann Stidman, Spirit Lake, Idaho

Some of my friends refer to this unbelievably rich ice cream dessert as "death by chocolate"—before they ask for seconds! It's a yummy, festive, do-ahead treat.

>   2 cups chocolate graham cracker crumbs
>   (about 32 squares)
>   1/2 cup butter, melted
>   1/2 cup chopped walnuts
>   1 tablespoon sugar
> FILLING:
>   1/2 gallon chocolate ice cream, softened
>   1 jar (12-1/4 ounces) caramel ice cream topping
>   1 jar (12-1/4 ounces) hot fudge ice cream topping
>   1/2 cup miniature semisweet chocolate chips
>   1/2 cup chopped walnuts
> TOPPING:
>   2 cups heavy whipping cream
>   3 tablespoons sugar
>   1 tablespoon baking cocoa
>   1 teaspoon vanilla extract
>   1/2 teaspoon instant coffee granules
> Additional miniature chocolate chips and chopped
>   walnuts

For crust, combine crumbs, butter, walnuts and sugar; press into an ungreased 13-in. x 9-in. x 2-in. baking pan. Bake at 350° for 10 minutes; cool completely.

Spread half of the ice cream over crust; spoon caramel and hot fudge toppings over ice cream. Sprinkle with chocolate chips and walnuts; freeze until firm. Spread remaining ice cream over the top. Cover with plastic wrap. Freeze for at least 2 hours.

In a mixing bowl, beat cream until stiff peaks form. Fold in sugar, cocoa, vanilla and coffee granules. Pipe or spoon onto dessert. Sprinkle with additional chocolate chips and walnuts. Return to the freezer until 10 minutes before serving. **Yield:** 16-20 servings.

PUMPKIN BREAD PUDDING
Lois Jamieson, Anaheim, California

Served warm or cold with a dollop of whipped cream, this old-fashioned treat is just like pumpkin pie without the crust.

>   3 eggs
> 1-3/4 cups canned pumpkin
> 1-1/2 cups milk
>   1 can (12 ounces) evaporated milk
>   1 cup sugar
>   2 tablespoons butter, melted
> 1-1/4 teaspoons ground cinnamon

1/2 teaspoon ground ginger, optional
1/2 teaspoon vanilla extract
1/4 teaspoon ground cloves
1/8 teaspoon ground nutmeg
6 slices bread, cubed
3/4 cup raisins
1/2 cup pecans, chopped
Whipped cream

In a large bowl, combine the eggs, pumpkin, milk, evaporated milk, sugar, butter, cinnamon, ginger if desired, vanilla, cloves and nutmeg. Add the bread cubes and raisins; mix well. Pour into a greased 11-in. x 7-in. x 2-in. baking dish. Sprinkle with pecans. Bake at 350° for 50-60 minutes or until a knife inserted near the center comes out clean. Serve with whipped cream. Refrigerate leftovers. **Yield:** 10 servings.

LAYERED POPPY SEED CAKE
Polly Manring, Chillicothe, Illinois

It's just not Christmas at our house until I bake and ice this old-time layer cake—my husband's favorite since he was a boy.

3/4 cup milk
1/3 cup poppy seeds
3/4 cup butter, softened
1-1/2 cups sugar
1-1/2 teaspoons vanilla extract
2 cups cake flour
2-1/2 teaspoons baking powder
1/4 teaspoon salt
4 egg whites
FILLING/TOPPING:
3/4 cup sugar
4-1/2 teaspoons cornstarch
6 egg yolks, lightly beaten
2-1/4 cups milk
1/4 cup chopped walnuts
1 teaspoon vanilla extract
Additional chopped walnuts and confectioners' sugar, optional

In a small bowl, combine milk and poppy seeds; let stand for 1 hour. In a large mixing bowl, cream butter and sugar. Beat in vanilla. Combine the flour, baking powder and salt; add to creamed mixture alternately with poppy seed mixture. In a small bowl, beat egg whites until stiff peaks form; fold into creamed mixture.

Spread into two greased and floured 8-in. round baking pans. Bake at 375° for 30-35 minutes or until a toothpick inserted near the center comes out clean. Cool for 10 minutes before removing from pans to wire racks to cool completely.

In a heavy saucepan, combine sugar and cornstarch. Combine egg yolks and milk; gradually stir into sugar mixture. Cook and stir over medium heat until mixture comes to a boil; cook and stir for 1-2 minutes or until thickened. Remove from the heat; cool completely. Stir in walnuts and vanilla.

Cut each cake layer horizontally in half. Place bottom layer on a serving plate; spread with a fourth of the filling. Repeat layers three times. Refrigerate for 2-3 hours. Garnish with additional walnuts and confectioners' sugar if desired. **Yield:** 12 servings.

CHRISTMAS TRIFLE
Esther McCoy, Dillonvale, Ohio
(Pictured above)

A flavorful blend of cake, pudding, eggnog and fruit will make folks think you really spent a lot of time putting together this fancy but fuss-free dessert.

1 can (8 ounces) crushed pineapple
3 medium firm bananas, sliced
1 jar (10 ounces) red maraschino cherries
1 jar (6 ounces) green maraschino cherries
3-1/2 cups eggnog*, chilled
2 packages (3.4 ounces *each*) instant vanilla pudding mix
1 prepared angel food cake (8 inches), cut into 1-inch cubes
1 carton (16 ounces) frozen whipped topping, thawed
1/4 cup chopped walnuts

Drain pineapple, reserving the juice. Dip bananas in juice; drain and discard juice. Set aside pineapple, bananas, three red cherries and three green cherries. In a bowl, whisk the eggnog and pudding mixes for 2 minutes or until slightly thickened.

Place half of the pudding in a 4-qt. serving or trifle bowl; layer with half of the bananas, pineapple, cherries, cake cubes and whipped topping. Repeat layers. Garnish with walnuts and reserved cherries. **Yield:** 16-20 servings.

*Editor's Note: This recipe was tested with commercially prepared eggnog.

Christmas Fantasy

Bake a Forest of Festive Yuletide Cookie Trees

FAMILY AND FRIENDS will agree it's beginning to look a lot like Christmas when they see the glistening treetops of this fanciful forest. Iced with creamy frosting and dusted with sparkly colored sugars, each of the 3-D cookie trees is as delicious as it is beautiful!

You can make the cookies in a variety of sizes to display on a mirrored surface or tiered on different levels. Or you might plant a stand in the center of your holiday table for a stunning centerpiece. The decorating possibilities are endless!

Our *CW* kitchen crew crafted the holly jolly treats that are sure to catch everyone's attention. You'll find the easy-to-follow directions right here, complete with helpful how-to photos at right. So go ahead and craft your own edible grove this December!

CHRISTMAS TREE COOKIES

1 cup butter, softened
1-1/4 cups sugar
2 eggs
2 teaspoons vanilla extract
3-1/2 cups all-purpose flour
2 teaspoons baking powder
Green gel *or* paste food coloring
FROSTING:
4-1/2 cups confectioners' sugar
1/2 cup warm water
3 tablespoons meringue powder
1 teaspoon vanilla extract
1/2 teaspoon cream of tartar
Green gel or paste food coloring
Assorted decorating sprinkles and white edible glitter

In a large mixing bowl, cream butter and sugar. Add eggs, one at a time, beating well after each addition. Beat in vanilla. Combine flour and baking powder; gradually add to creamed mixture. Divide dough in half. Tint half of the dough green; knead well to distribute color evenly. Leave remaining dough white. Cover and refrigerate for 1 hour or until easy to handle.

On a lightly floured surface, roll out each portion of dough to 1/8-in. thickness. Use tree-shaped cookie cutters with identical shapes, measuring 2-1/2 in., 3 in., 4 in. and 4-1/2 in. Cut out an even number of cookies with each size cookie cutter. Place 1 in. apart on ungreased baking sheets.

Bake at 350° for 8-10 minutes or until golden brown. Immediately cut half of each size tree cookies in half from top to bottom. If tree cookie cutters have trunks, trim trunks off trees, creating a flat base. Remove to wire racks to cool.

For frosting, combine the confectioners' sugar, water, meringue powder, vanilla and cream of tartar in a large mixing bowl. Beat on high speed for 8-10 minutes or until stiff peaks form. Divide frosting in half. Tint half of the frosting green; leave remaining frosting white. Cover frosting with damp paper towels or plastic wrap between uses.

To make four-sided garland trees (on top in photo at left): Cut a small hole in the corner of a pastry or resealable plastic bag; insert round pastry tip #5. Fill with green or white frosting to match the tree you are decorating. Pipe a line of frosting along the cut edge of one of the halved cookies (see Photo 1); press frosted edge along center of a matching whole cookie. Repeat. Let dry until firm.

Stand up partially assembled trees. Attach one matching cookie half to the opposite side of the tree by piping frosting along cut edge and pressing along center of whole cookie (see Photo 2). Let dry completely.

Using another pastry or resealable plastic bag, medium star pastry tip #21 and either white or green frosting, pipe garlands around sides of trees. Decorate with sprinkles if desired. Let dry completely.

To make fuller trees (top right and lower left in photo at left): Assemble trees as described for four-sided garland trees, using white or green cookies. Using matching colored frosting, attach four cookie halves, one size smaller than assembled tree cookies. Let trees dry completely. Decorate using either the garland or snow-tipped technique. Dry completely.

To make snow-tipped trees (at lower left in photo at left): Assemble trees as described for fuller trees using green cookies. Using another pastry or resealable plastic bag, large round pastry tip #8 and white frosting, pipe snow on tips of branches. Sprinkle with edible glitter. Let dry completely.

To make glazed trees (at lower right in photo at left): In a small bowl, thin 1 cup green frosting with 2-3 tablespoons water until frosting reaches

pourable consistency. Place matching pairs of whole and halved cookies on a wire rack over waxed paper. Pour icing over cookies; spread with a metal spatula to completely cover top and sides of cookies. Let dry completely. Assemble, using garland tree method; let dry. Decorate as desired. **Yield:** 6 dozen cookies (or 18-36 cookie trees, depending on fullness of trees.)

*Editor's Note: Meringue powder, edible glitter and tree cookie cutter sets can be ordered by mail from Wilton Industries, Inc. Call 1-800/794-5866 or visit their Web site, *www.wilton.com*.

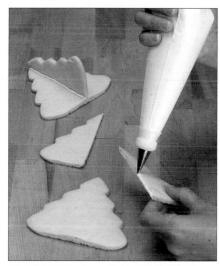

Photo 1. Pipe a line of frosting along the cut edge of one of the halved cookies. Carefully press the frosted edge along the center line of a matching whole cookie. Let dry until firm.

Photo 2. Stand up partially assembled trees. Pipe a line of frosting along the cut edge of a second matching cookie half. Press the frosted edge onto the center of the whole cookie, opposite the first cookie half.

 # Let It Snow

By Lori Ness of Cambridge, Minnesota

"SMILE! You love parties," said Nathan, slipping his arm around my waist and waltzing me around the room. "You can dance all night, Sal. That's why I married you."

"I thought you married me because I could dance all night, rise at 5 a.m., sit on a tractor for 9 hours straight and still have enough energy to inoculate a batch of piglets," I replied.

"No, it was the dancing," he grinned.

I let him hold me close, but my lengthy "to do" list kept popping into my mind—vacuum the carpet, clean up cereal the kids had spilled…

Rubbing my back, Nathan soothed, "Relax, hon. The house looks great, and this is just a family party. Everyone would be happy with hot dogs."

"Well, I wouldn't! I want this evening to be perfect so the boys have special memories of family get-togethers. But I've got a hundred things to do."

Nathan let me go. "How about a fire tonight, Sal? Everyone always enjoys a crackling blaze."

"And what about all the ashes and soot? We're having an elegant buffet, not a marshmallow roast."

"I love marshmallows," piped up Josiah, beaming.

"We're not serving marshmallows," I informed my son crisply, then turned to Nathan.

"Try to understand, darling. This party is our family tradition. I want the house to look its best."

He gave me a hug and headed off to work on repairing a tractor, our three sons in tow. I dashed off to attack the remaining items on my list.

But a strange heaviness weighed on me as I fed the chickens and checked on the colt. My head ached as I cut out cookies and scrubbed the kitchen floor. Sighing, I massaged my throbbing temples. Was I getting sick?

I'd just started to tie red bows around rolled linen napkins when the boys reappeared, bubbling with excitement.

"It's snowing, Mom!" crowed Ryan, nose and hands pressed against the window. He wriggled like a puppy. "Can we go out and play?"

"Please, Mom!" Josiah and Kyle chimed in. "It would be so much fun!"

But who had time for fun with a party to put on?

"Absolutely not! You'll make a mess and track in snow. Read a book or play a quiet game," I ordered.

Their faces fell and they trudged away, shoulders drooping, while I tackled the window Ryan had smeared.

I busily sprayed window cleaner as the radio played *Joy to the World.*

"There's no joy in this house," I muttered, feeling woefully unappreciated.

And then I stopped, towel raised to wipe away the last handprint. What was I doing? All my fussing and fretting had taken the "merry" out of our Christmas!

I gazed at the steadily falling snow, heart aching, and suddenly thought about my mother. She'd been gone more than 10 years, but I still missed her so.

Mother had reveled in snow—blizzards or flurries. I remember watching her smile as flakes fell on her upturned face and powdered her hair.

Using my apron to wipe away a tear, I recalled those Christmas mornings when my sister and I were awakened early by Mother warbling, "Let it snow, let it snow, let it snow!"

Giggling with excitement, we'd jump out of bed and into our snowsuits, hurrying outside to build a snow manger and a Baby Jesus to lay in it.

Afterward, mittens soaked and noses red with cold, we'd tumble into the heavenly warmth of the kitchen.

I blinked back more tears as I pictured that kitchen, cluttered but cozy, a pile of boots and mittens near the door.

I shook my head in disbelief at my own blindness. Outside, the snow continued to fall. It wasn't too late!

Nathan entered the room. "Is there something I can do to help you get ready, honey?"

I ripped up my "to do" list and laughed. "You could start by making hot chocolate. Enough for all of us."

My husband blinked. "Hot chocolate? What about the buffet?"

"I've decided on hot dogs. We can roast them in the fireplace. A fire is so delightful when the weather outside is frightful."

"Think maybe you've been listening to too many carols?" mumbled a dumbfounded Nathan. But he laughed when I hurried, with a song in my heart, to find my precious children.

"Boys!" I hollered. "Get your snow pants and coats on. We've got some snowmen and memories to make!"

Organize Holiday Baking With A List Worth Checking Twice

By Kathy Ingrao of West Lafayette, Indiana

HAVE YOU HAD your fill of lists at Christmas? I know I was finding my long litanies of "Things To Do" disheartening. But then, in the process of doing my Christmas baking, I came up with a different and far more encouraging kind of list.

Now, my "Things I Did" list also serves as a kind of personal advice column for the holiday baking that I love to do but used to have trouble finding time for.

This year, try cooking up your very own "Things I Did" list as you begin your baking, and see how useful it is next year. Here are some tips to get you going.

• Write down when you start your holiday baking. For instance, I noted "started about 10 days ahead and was able to make quite a variety of treats during those 10 days."

Traditions to Try

IT'S FUNNY how simple customs, repeated often enough—or sometimes only once—can become treasured family traditions at Christmas! Try initiating some of your own family traditions this holiday season:

☆ Have the children write their letters to Santa on the same date every year, say St. Nicholas' Day. Then slip them into a paper stocking hanging at the fireplace for his elves to collect. Don't *you* forget to check the lists twice before shopping...then save them for your scrapbook!

☆ Tuck a box of "thank you" cards in each child's stocking. Then set aside time on New Year's Day for them to write (or draw) a thank-you to relatives for gifts they received.

☆ 'Tis the season to bring out family photo albums and holiday snaps. Keep them handy for friends and family to enjoy.

In future Christmas seasons, if I'm behind on my cards or have lots of last-minute shopping to do, I might want to begin baking earlier and rely on my freezer a bit more.

• List each recipe you make—and, if it's a new one, note the cookbook it came from. Should it prove to be a hit with your family, you'll want to make the new treat again next year. Think how glad you'll be when you don't have to leaf through book after book wondering where that recipe came from!

• Make a note of individual family-member favorites. I tried a butterscotch fudge recipe one year that my daughter loved. Now I know the way to her heart every Christmas. (If you'd like to try a similar recipe, we've included one for Butterscotch Fudge at right.)

• Compliment yourself. If those little wreath cookies with the tinted icing turned out to be especially pretty, write that down. Next year, when you reread the list, you'll give yourself a smile of appreciation!

• Record your disappointments. The chocolate fudge I made this year set fine, but the pieces were too thin. Next year I'll remember to make a double recipe for the same size pan so I get thick, irresistible squares of fudge.

• Caution yourself. If those candy cane cookies took hours to shape and then melted into unrecognizable blobs in the oven, don't repeat the same mistake next year. Make a note to vary your shaping technique or scratch them off your list. Not every recipe is worth repeating. Next year, you'll want to try some new ones.

• Encourage yourself. The last note on last year's list really should have been the first: "Gingerbread house—baked the week of December 8th (as a surprise for my children while they were at school) and assembled on the 14th—beautiful!"

I had always wanted to make a gingerbread house and last year, I finally did. I'm sure I won't repeat the performance every single year, but knowing the timetable I used and the success I had will encourage me to try it again.

BUTTERSCOTCH FUDGE
(Pictured above)

1-1/2 teaspoons plus 1/2 cup butter (no substitutes), softened, *divided*
2 cups packed brown sugar
1 cup sugar
1 cup evaporated milk
1 jar (7 ounces) marshmallow creme
1/3 cup peanut butter
1 teaspoon vanilla extract
1 cup butterscotch chips

Line a 9-in. square pan with foil and grease the foil with 1-1/2 teaspoons butter; set aside. In a large heavy saucepan, combine the sugars, milk and remaining butter. Cook and stir over medium heat until sugar is dissolved. Bring to a rapid boil; boil for 5 minutes, stirring constantly. Reduce heat to low; stir in the marshmallow creme and peanut butter until melted and blended.

Remove from the heat; stir in vanilla. Add the butterscotch chips; stir until chips are melted. Pour into prepared pan. Refrigerate for 4 hours or until firm. Using foil, remove fudge from pan; carefully peel off foil. Store in refrigerator. **Yield: 2-3/4 pounds.**

Welcome To My Country Kitchen

By Linda Salonen of Dryden, Ontario

A CHRISTMAS DREAM come true…that's how I like to think of my spacious country kitchen. There's simply *nothing* about this room that I don't love, especially when it's all trimmed for the season and our four children and two granddaughters come home to celebrate the holiday.

This kitchen has everything—a large walk-in pantry with loads of outlets for appliances…a bay window and hinged window seat with beautiful views and hidden storage…and the handy adjacent laundry room.

It was my husband, Bill, a retired teacher, who stumbled across the perfect floor plan while paging through an issue of *Country Woman* years ago. We were planning the home we wanted to build on the banks of the Wabigoon River.

"This is the kitchen I want," he said firmly, pointing to photos in the Nov/Dec 1997 edition of the holiday-decked kitchen of Jim and Rose Ryczkowski of De Pere, Wisconsin. And that's the kitchen we have today—thanks to that couple's help.

Merry Mirror Image

Like Rose, I have a tiny Christmas village nestled on snowy batting in the recessed window over my kitchen sink. (The twinkling lights are so lovely at night!) My cabinets are also topped with bow-tied evergreen garlands and sprinkled with spicy homemade gingerbread boys. Even our floor covering is the same diamond-patterned linoleum as Rose and Jim's— only with green accents instead of their blue ones.

And we received an added Christmas bonus. We've become fast friends with this cordial couple and have visited their home several times. Last December, Rose even sent us some of her delicious homemade pickles and jam!

If friends and family are what this special season is all

TRIMMED IN HOLLY and gingerbread, the Ontario kitchen of Linda Salonen (above left) reflects the spirit of the season and her own crafting abilities. She made the little flowerpot angels that top the canisters below and also the many fur-trimmed Santa figures throughout the house.

about, then my kitchen is truly a celebration of both. Preparation, cooking and eating areas all blend into one big, bright airy room, reminding me of the farmhouse kitchen that held so many of my own happy childhood memories.

Our central island, which features a handy hidden recycling center, is the first place visitors stop to sit down, share a cup of coffee and chat.

It's also where my two granddaughters like to color, do crafts and help me build the gingerbread house that's our special tradition every December.

Once our scraps are cleared away, however, my Precious Moments Nativity set takes center stage on the island—all except for Baby Jesus.

We wait until just before the girls go to bed on Christmas Eve to tuck the baby in his manger.

Home Sweet Holidays

In the morning, we're up early to open gifts, then the whole brood gathers for a festive breakfast of strawberry crepes, sausages and orange juice.

Decked only in valances, our big windows let in all the sunshine and stunning views of the snowy river, glistening treetops and wildlife that fill our yard. Inside, seasonal tea towels, throw rugs, knickknacks and my own crafts dress our kitchen in true holiday style.

As a retired family studies teacher, I've always loved trying my hand at painting and different homespun crafts. You'll see my fur-trimmed Santa figures scattered throughout the rooms and my homemade ornaments that decorate our tree.

But it's for our festive Yuletide dinner that I really pull out all the stops. I turn to red table linens, candles, bright bows for the cabinets, special Noel dinnerware and, of course, our traditional turkey with all the fancy fixin's.

Later in the evening, we might gather around the table again after skating on the river to share cocoa and cookies. Or we might sing a few carols before putting the holiday to bed.

It's been a delight showing you around the kitchen that we dress up and enjoy so much for the holidays.

But to tell the truth, we spend more time in this room year-round than any other in the house. Maybe that's because it has a kind of built-in family feeling—a way of bringing to mind dear friends, good times and a lingering wisp of true Christmas spirit any time of year at all.

Happy Holidays!

YULETIDE REMINDERS of the real reason for the season are easy to find throughout the Salonens' holiday household. Their treasured Precious Moments Nativity scene (above) is only one of many Christmas traditions that Linda brings out every December to celebrate this warm and wonderful time with her family. She also gathers granddaughters in her cheery kitchen to concoct an annual gingerbread house and helps make spirits bright with her festive turkey dinner.

Living Christmas Card

The brilliant lights that twinkle
On the countless wintry trees…
The manger scenes with wise men
And the shepherds on their knees…
The candles in the windows…
All leave Christmas memories.

To see the luminaries
As they march across a yard…
To walk about and revel
In the heavens, thickly starred…
Is to find oneself a figure
In a living Christmas card.

—Isabelle Farnham
Boulder, Colorado

Grandma's Brag Page

MAKING *MMM*MERRY with sugar and spice and everything nice are 10-month-old triplets Madison, Regan and Sarah Lammers. "They triple the holiday spirit for us all," says a laughing Jackie Hillman of Belgrade, Montana about her sugar-dusted, elf-size granddaughters.

SANTA'S LITTLE HELPER, pretty 3-year-old Stephanie, is the Christmas joy of her grandma Linda Sobolewski in Macomb, Michigan.

SEEING IS BELIEVING. Her grandson Alex is checkin' old St. Nick out twice, writes Gerry Alenius from Greendale, Wisconsin.

TIDINGS OF GREAT JOY. "Our seven grandchildren and the pet donkey got together to pose for this Christmas-card rendition of *Silent Night*," writes Grandma Faye Anderson of Bowden, Alberta. "Believe me, though, the night of that photo shoot was neither silent nor calm!"

AWAY IN A MANGER. Her grandkids, Becka and baby brother Trent Bruntz (in swaddling clothes), couldn't be much sweeter as a pint-size Madonna and Child, writes Eileen Kohmetscher from Lawrence, Nebraska. "They brighten every Christmas."

HAUL OUT THE HOLLY... Little Carli-Marie Maybuck and her trusty dog "Shelby" are all dolled up and ready to celebrate a merry first Christmas with "Grammie" Olga Maybuck and the rest of the family at her home in Battleford, Saskatchewan!

CUSTOM-MADE FOR CHRISTMAS. Beautifully trimmed wreaths, ropes or garlands made to any length needed, plus acres of cut-your-own balsams are the Vermont specialty of Polly Wilson.

Lasting Holiday Memories Trim These Vermont Balsams

HAPPY HOLIDAYS—and the evergreen memories they inspire—do grow on trees at Wilson's Tree Farm outside rural Putney in southeast Vermont.

"We wanted a place where families could enjoy that old-time tradition of hiking through snowy woods in search of the perfect Christmas tree," explains Polly Wilson.

"But believe me," she adds with a laugh, "perfect means something different to everyone.

"Some people like their tree short and fat; others prefer a tall skinny one that can fit in a corner. Some seek a thick, bushy pine to fill an entire room; others want the 'Charlie Brown' look to display their ornaments better."

Fortunately, there's a tree for everyone, Polly believes.

She started the business with her late husband, Steve, nearly a quarter of a century ago on 10 acres of their 130-acre hillside farm. The rest of the land is managed forest that has provided the

family with logs for lumber, firewood for heat, maple trees for sugaring and a rich wildlife habitat.

An older son and daughter are grown and on their own, but Benjamin, 13, lives at home and helps with the business.

"We used to sell precut trees, but now it's all cut-your-own balsams so no trees are wasted," Polly says. "Of course, we're glad to cut down a tree for people who come without the equipment or inclination to do it themselves."

She uses a handy baler to wrap the tree neatly in plastic netting and says, "That simple process makes the trees so much easier to transport, people often put two in their car. Once they're home and in the stand, a snip of plastic netting…and everything falls into place!"

Christmas is part of Polly's life all year long. January finds her ordering new trees to transplant in spring. With

that planting comes fertilizing and constant mowing to keep weeds down.

"By fall, the new growth has hardened off. It's time to prune the trees and start getting ready for our busy season," she explains.

Polly goes to great lengths to keep customers merry, creating garlands anywhere from 3 feet to 120 feet and hundreds of her one-of-a-kind wreaths. She twists every bow and trims every wreath herself, using pinecones, berries, statice, greens, mushrooms, even special themes if asked.

Families find a Christmas wonderland at Wilson's Tree Farm, with homemade cookies, warm mulled cider and carols in the air. They may come for a holiday tree, but they'll leave with holiday memories to last a lifetime.

Editor's Note: *For more information on Wilson's Tree Farm mail-order wreaths and garlands, E-mail Polly at Treefarm@sovernet or phone 1-802/387-8757.*

Fill Your Christmas Gifts with Fun!

IF SHOPPING crowded malls for all the names on your list is turning you into a basket case, think gift baskets!

With a little creativity on your part, simple staples, toiletries and presents from the pantry can be transformed into a delightfully personal, one-of-a-kind gift that will be remembered with special warmth the whole year through.

Gift baskets can be easily tailored to any age, situation or theme. Plus, they make a dazzling presentation with just a little colored cellophane and some bright ribbon.

Brainy Idea

Why not beat the holiday rush and treat far-flung college-age kids or nephews and nieces to an early care package? It'll help get them through exams and into a holiday spirit!

We used tissue paper in school colors to wrap up a string of Yuletide lights for decking the dorm room, Christmas music CDs, some toasty holiday socks, tins of cocoa mix and flavored tea bags.

Also tucked inside are a stuffed school mascot, Christmas cards (for teachers and school friends) and a container of holiday cookies and sweets big enough to share with a roommate!

Aged to Perfection

For Grandma or older relatives, our gift basket comes brimful of goodies sure to satisfy all their senses!

There are a pair of warm fuzzy slippers, crossword puzzle books and an easy-to-grip ballpoint pen, a bag of holiday-scented potpourri and a pinecone-trimmed candle, Christmas notes and stamps, tiny jars of jam and jelly, peppermint and chamomile tea and a big tin of home-baked treats.

To tailor a similar basket to Grandpa, you can include a magazine or newspaper subscription, favorite movies, soaps and shaving cream, a natty Christmas tie or socks and a tin of salted nuts or old-time ribbon candy.

Making the Grade

Show appreciation to a favorite teacher with a small well-stocked basket. Fill it with a spicy clove-studded orange pomander (your child could easily make this), a shiny apple paperweight for her desk, a festive garland, candy-cane candle, Christmas thank-you cards, cranberry tea and a mug filled with holiday sweets.

Or remember a special friend's thoughtfulness with a basket filled to the brim with soothing stress-relievers. Soap and body lotion in her favorite scent will help wash away winter's sting, and sachets to tuck in her closet or drawer will remind her of your warm appreciation.

And for a luxurious soak in the tub that Santa himself would envy, add a CD of relaxing music, bath salts, small candles or tea lights, a rejuvenating loofah scrub, scented lotion, eye shades and comforting herbal tea.

Finally, make your favorite hound an official member of the family with his own little basket. Fill it up with a fun food dish, stuffed and squeaky toys in bright colors, a sturdy new leather leash and some rawhide chews or crunchy doggy treats.

Or try making up a similar basket for the cat of a hard-to-buy-for friend! 🎄

Traditions to Try

THE LATE Fred Rogers of PBS' beloved *Mister Rogers' Neighborhood* once noted: "The way you celebrate Christmas can be a gift in itself, handing on traditions that will give your child a feeling of continuity, comfort and joy in all the Christmases to come." Give your family the gift of traditions!

❋ Make a family Christmas tape and record each member singing a carol, making a Christmas wish, mentioning a favorite holiday moment or memory. Add to the tape each year.

❋ Collect Christmas books for all ages and bring them out every year to enjoy together over the holiday season. Encourage older kids to pick a personal favorite to read to younger siblings.

A-TISKET, A-TASKET... Put together some creative holiday gift baskets for special friends and relatives or just to keep on hand as last-minute gifts for unannounced visitors or neighbors! Select baskets that will be useful, too—maybe to store craft supplies, hold magazines or organize letters on a desktop.

Craft Section

Deck Your Walls With Winsome Winter Welcome

PATCH TOGETHER a happy holiday gift with this charming 8-inch-square wall hanging from Jeanne Prue of Newport, Vermont. The friendly little snowman and bright feathered friend will melt the hearts—and warm the winters!—of all who see them.

"You could also use this down-home applique to decorate sweatshirts, hot pads and other items," Jeanne suggests.

Materials Needed:
Patterns on next page
1/8 yard of paper-backed fusible web
Pencil
44-inch-wide 100% cotton fabrics—3/8 yard of red print for hatband and bird appliques, binding and backing; 1/8 yard each or scraps of green print for border and red-and-green plaid for hanging tabs and scarf; 8-inch square of blue mottled fabric for background; and scraps each of black for hat, orange for nose and white-on-white print for snowman
All-purpose thread to match fabrics
Tear-away stabilizer or typing paper
8-inch square of lightweight quilt batting
Three 1/4-inch dark green buttons
Two 1/2-inch red four-hole buttons
One 5/8-inch red star-shaped button
Powdered cosmetic blush
Cotton swab
Quilter's ruler
Quilter's marking pen or pencil
Rotary cutter and mat (optional)
Black fine-line permanent marker
Standard sewing supplies
6-inch decorative wire star hanger or 6-inch length of 1/4-inch wooden dowel

Finished Size: Snowman wall hanging is 8 inches square without hanger and hanging tabs.

Directions:
Hand-wash all fabrics without fabric softeners, washing colors separately. If the water from any fabric is discolored, wash again until rinse water runs clear. Dry and press all fabrics.

CUTTING: Either use marking pen and ruler to mark the fabrics before cutting pieces with a scissors or use rotary cutting tools to cut the pieces as directed in the instructions that follow. Cut the strips crosswise from selvage to selvage.

From blue mottled fabric, cut a 6-1/2-in. square for background.

From green print, cut two 1-1/2-in. x 6-1/2-in. strips and two 1-1/2-in. x 8-in. strips for border.

From red-and-green plaid, cut one 2-1/2-in. x 6-1/2-in. strip for hanging tabs and one 7/8-in. x 4-1/2-in. strip for scarf.

From red print, cut one 8-in. square for backing and one 1-1/2-in. x 38-in. strip for binding.

APPLIQUES: Trace each individual applique pattern, including overlapped portions of patterns and grain lines, onto paper side of fusible web, leaving 1/2 in. between shapes. Cut out shapes, leaving a margin of paper around each.

Following manufacturer's directions, fuse shapes onto wrong side of fabrics as directed on patterns. When cool, cut out each shape.

Remove paper backing from shapes. Referring to photo and pattern, position snowman on right side of background fabric with bottom edges even. Add remaining shapes as shown.

Before fusing shapes in place, fringe edges of red-and-green scarf fabric strip. Fold piece in half at a slight angle and tuck fold under bottom edge of scarf applique. Fuse shapes in place.

Place tear-away stabilizer or typing paper behind appliques.

Using matching thread and a medium satin stitch, applique around each shape in the following order: Snowman, nose, hat, hatband, bird and scarf. Remove stabilizer or typing paper. Bring all loose threads to back and secure.

BORDER: Do all stitching with right sides together, edges even, matching thread and accurate 1/4-in. seams. Press seams toward the darker fabric unless instructions say otherwise.

Sew a 6-1/2-in.-long green print border to opposite sides of the appliqued block. Open and press.

Sew an 8-1/2-in.-long green print border to top and bottom of appliqued block. Open and press.

QUILTING: Place backing fabric wrong side up on a flat surface. Center

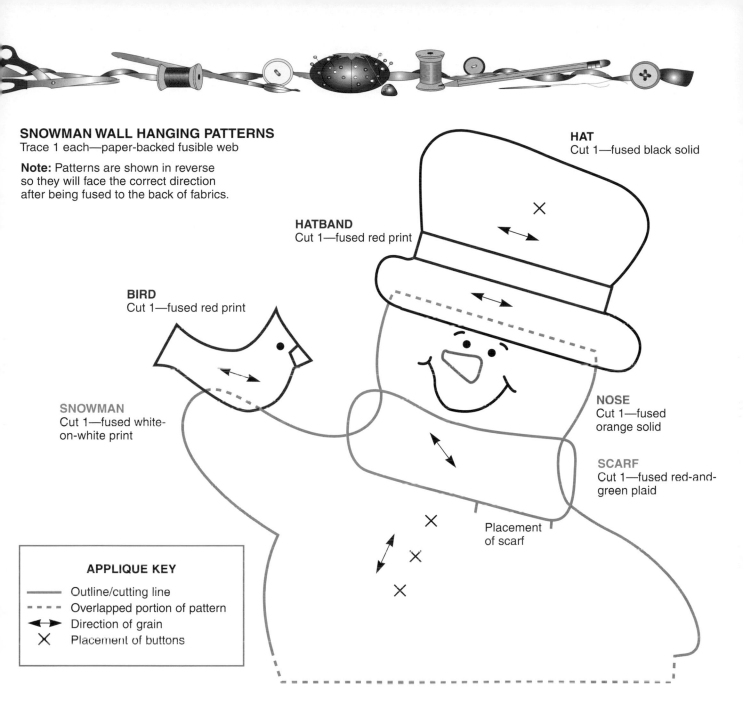

SNOWMAN WALL HANGING PATTERNS
Trace 1 each—paper-backed fusible web

Note: Patterns are shown in reverse so they will face the correct direction after being fused to the back of fabrics.

HAT
Cut 1—fused black solid

HATBAND
Cut 1—fused red print

BIRD
Cut 1—fused red print

SNOWMAN
Cut 1—fused white-on-white print

NOSE
Cut 1—fused orange solid

SCARF
Cut 1—fused red-and-green plaid

Placement of scarf

APPLIQUE KEY

——— Outline/cutting line

- - - - Overlapped portion of pattern

←→ Direction of grain

✕ Placement of buttons

batting on top of backing. Center appliqued block right side up on top of batting. Baste layers together, stitching a scant 1/4 in. from outer edges.

BINDING: Trim one short end of binding strip diagonally. Press trimmed end and one long edge 1/4 in. to the wrong side.

Sew binding to front of quilt with raw edges matching and a 1/4-in. seam, mitering corners (see Figs. 1 and 2) and overlapping the ends. Trim excess binding. Fold binding to back of quilt, encasing raw edges and mitering corners. Hand-sew the fold of binding to backing, covering machine-stitching on back.

HANGING TABS: Fold all raw edges of a 2-1/2-in. x 6-1/2-in. red-and-green plaid strip 1/4 in. to wrong side and press.

Fold strip in half lengthwise with wrong sides together. Topstitch around, stitching as close as possible to edges.

If desired, machine-sew a lengthwise buttonhole at each short end.

Cut stitched piece in half to make two 1-in. x 3-in. tabs. Fold raw edges under and pin each hanging tab to top of back of wall hanging with side edges about 1 in. from sides of wall hanging. Hand-tack fold of tabs to the back of the wall hanging.

FINISHING: With matching thread and stitching through all layers, hand-sew green buttons to snowman and star button to hat where shown on the patterns.

Fold hanging tabs to front and mark buttonhole placement on top border. Using matching thread and stitch-

through all layers, hand-sew the two four-hole buttons to border.

Use black marker to add eyes, eyebrows and mouth where shown on pattern.

Use cotton swab and a circular motion to apply blush to cheeks.

Add wire hanger or wooden dowel; button tabs in place.   ⊛

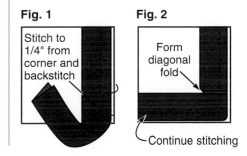

Fig. 1
Stitch to 1/4" from corner and backstitch

Fig. 2
Form diagonal fold

Continue stitching

Make the Christmas Story a Joyful Showstopper!

LOOKING FOR a way to showcase the *real* reason for the season with youngsters? Try this inspiring Nativity stage set with pint-size finger puppets from Verlyn King of Tremonton, Utah.

Materials Needed:
Patterns on next page
Tracing paper and pencil
Felt—one 9-inch x 12-inch piece of black glitter felt for stage; two 9-inch x 12-inch pieces of tan for stage floor; two 2-inch x 3-inch pieces each of white, light blue, light brown, gray, orange, dark green and lavender felt for each puppet; and scraps of black, dark brown, charcoal gray, cranberry, cream, medium blue, soft beige, tan and white
All-purpose thread to match felt for puppets
Scraps of dark brown, dark green, purple, gold, green, cranberry and yellow yarn
Ten 3/4-inch wooden spools (optional for standing figures)
Black fine-line permanent marker
3-inch length of gold-and-white pipe cleaner (chenille stem)
Wire cutters
2-inch length of jute string
4-inch length of green metallic trim
1/16-inch-thick x 1-inch-high wooden star (Verlyn used a small Woodsies star)
Wooden craft pick or 4-inch length of wooden skewer
Round and star-shaped sequins in assorted colors and one large gold star sequin
7-1/2-inch-wide x 10-3/4-inch-tall x 2-3/8-inch-deep lightweight cardboard box (Verlyn used a cereal box)
Ruler
Craft knife
Foam plate or palette
Paper towels
Black acrylic craft paint
1-inch foam brush
Toothpick
White (tacky) glue
Standard sewing supplies

Finished Size: Stage is 7-1/2 inches tall x 10-3/4 inches wide x 2-3/8 inches deep when closed. When opened, stage is 7-1/2 inches tall x 10-3/4 inches wide x 13 inches deep. The donkey and camel puppets each measure about 2 inches across x 2-3/4 inches tall. Mary, Joseph, shepherds and wise men all measure 1-1/2 inches across x 2-3/4 inches tall.

Directions:
PUPPETS: Trace patterns onto tracing paper as directed on patterns.

Cut puppets from felt as directed on patterns.

Pin two matching pieces of felt together with edges matching. With matching thread, machine-sew around curved edge, stitching through both layers about 1/8 in. from outside edge. Repeat for remaining figures.

Cut remaining shapes from felt as directed on patterns. Cut out and discard shaded area of each beard/hair piece.

Refer to patterns and photo for positioning felt pieces and trims on puppets.

Use toothpick to apply glue to small pieces. Let glue dry after each addition.

Angel: Glue a cream puppet face and two matching hands to one side of a white felt puppet.

Cut two 1-in. lengths of yellow yarn. Glue to opposite sides of face for hair.

Cut two 1/2-in. lengths of gold-and-white pipe cleaner. Glue a piece to the end of each hand.

Cut a 2-in. length of gold-and-white pipe cleaner. Glue piece across top of head for halo, wrapping excess to back.

Glue a large gold star sequin between hands.

Mary: Glue a cream puppet face to one side of a light blue felt puppet.

Glue a piece of dark brown yarn around sides and top of face for hair.

Glue baby to same side of Mary. Glue baby's face to baby's body.

Glue two cream hands to Mary, overlapping hands onto baby.

Cut two 1/2-in. x 1/8-in. pieces of medium blue felt for trim. Glue a felt trim piece to the end of each hand.

Joseph: Glue a cream puppet face and two matching hands to one side of a light brown felt puppet.

Cut two 1/2-in. lengths of purple yarn. Glue a yarn piece to end of each hand.

Glue black beard/hair to face.

Cut a 1-in. length of purple yarn. Glue piece of purple yarn across top of beard/hair.

Shepherds: Glue a cream puppet face and two matching hands to one side of each gray felt puppet.

Cut two 1/2-in. lengths each of dark green and cranberry yarn. Glue a dark green piece to the end of each hand of one shepherd. Repeat with cranberry yarn on other shepherd.

Cut a 1-in. length each of jute string, dark green yarn and cranberry yarn. Glue a jute string across the top of each shepherd's beard/hair. Glue cranberry yarn piece above jute string of shepherd with cranberry trim on hands; and dark green yarn piece above jute string of shepherd with dark green trim on hands.

Glue two small black felt pieces to opposite sides of one shepherd's face for hair.

Glue a piece of dark brown yarn around sides and top of face of other shepherd for hair. Glue a lamb between hands of each shepherd.

Wise men: Glue a soft beige puppet

face to one side of a dark green, lavender and orange puppet.

Glue a gray beard/hair over the face of the green wise man, a black beard/hair over the face of the lavender wise man and brown beard/hair over the face of the orange wise man.

Glue the box, small bottle and large bottle to the wise men as desired. Then glue two soft beige hands to each puppet.

Cut a 1-in. length each of green and gold yarn and green metallic trim. Glue yarn and trim pieces across the top of the beard/hair of each wise man.

Cut a 1/2-in. piece each of gold yarn and green metallic trim. Glue yarn and trim pieces to ends of hands, matching the trim on each.

Glue sequins to small and large bottles and box as desired.

Donkey and camel: Glue donkey to front of remaining white puppet and camel to remaining light blue puppet.

Finishing: Use black marker to add eyes, nose and mouth to each puppet.

Use black marker to add an eye, nose, ear and hooves to each lamb.

If desired, insert spools into the bottom of each to make puppets stand.

STAGE: Cutting: Glue openings of box closed. Let dry.

To make opening for front stage floor, measure and mark a line 1-1/8 in. from each narrow end of box and another line 1-1/2 in. from one long side of box. See Fig. 1. Use craft knife and ruler to cut along the three marked lines.

To make opening for back stage floor, measure and mark a line 1 in. from each narrow end on opposite side of box and another line 3 in. from long side of box. See Fig. 2. Cut along the three marked lines as before.

Painting: Paint as directed, applying additional coats of paint as needed for complete coverage. Let paint dry after every application.

Paint inside of box black, including flaps for stage floors. When dry, paint entire outside of box.

Stage floors: Cut two 1/2-in.-wide x 2-in.-long pieces of tan felt. Fold each felt strip in half crosswise with ends matching. Glue one folded felt strip centered along the edge of the front stage floor and the other one centered along the edge of the back stage floor.

Cut a piece of tan felt the same size as the front stage floor. Glue felt to stage floor with edges matching, taking care not to cover the crease with felt.

In the same way, cut and glue a piece of tan felt to the back stage floor and to the inside stage floor.

Outside stage wall: Measure and cut a piece of black glitter felt to fit front outside stage wall (around front stage opening). Glue felt to the box with edges matching.

Glue small star sequins randomly to outside stage wall.

Inside stage wall: Measure and cut a piece of black glitter felt to fit the back inside stage wall (around the inside back stage opening). Glue felt to box with edges matching. Glue small sequins randomly to inside back stage wall.

Star: Paint craft pick or wooden skewer and one side of wooden star black.

Glue sequins to unpainted side of star, covering completely. Glue craft pick or skewer to painted side of star. Use scissors to make a small hole in the top center of stage. Insert end of craft pick or skewer into hole with sequin side of star facing the front. ⊕

CRECHE FINGER PUPPET PATTERNS
Trace 1 each—tracing paper

GIFTS

PUPPET FACE
Cut 5—cream felt
Cut 3—soft beige felt

PUPPET
Cut 4 each—gray, light blue and white felt
Cut 2 each—light brown, dark green, lavender and orange felt

LARGE BOTTLE
Cut 1—medium blue felt

BOX
Cut 1—tan felt

SMALL BOTTLE
Cut 1—cranberry felt

DONKEY
Cut 1—charcoal felt

BEARD/HAIR
Cut 1 each—dark brown and gray felt
Cut 2—black felt

HAND
Cut 10—cream felt
Cut 6—soft beige felt

BABY'S FACE
Cut 1—cream felt

BABY
Cut 1—white felt

LAMB
Cut 2—white felt

CAMEL
Cut 1—dark brown felt

Fig. 1 Cutting opening for front stage floor

1-1/2 in.

1-1/8 in.   1-1/8 in.

Fig. 2 Cutting opening for back stage floor

3 in.

1 in.   1 in.

Stockings Hung with Care Put Best Foot Forward for St. Nick

SANTA HIMSELF will chuckle out loud when he spots these adorable stockings waiting to be filled with Yuletide goodies!

Sheryl Radakovich of Portage, Indiana whipped up the winsome doll and "endeering" Rudolph using bright felt appliques and some holiday accents.

"The stockings are so easy to make," says Sheryl. "And they're put together with embroidery floss so you don't even need a sewing machine."

Materials Needed (for both):
Patterns on next page and page 68.
Tracing paper and pencil
Black six-strand embroidery floss
Embroidery needle
Black and red dimensional fabric/craft paint
Straight pins
White (tacky) glue
Scissors

Additional Materials Needed (for doll stocking):
Felt—two 10-inch x 15-inch pieces of red for stocking; and one 9-inch x 12-inch piece or scraps each of dark green for cuff, slip and heart, blue for dress, brown for hair, off-white for face, hands and legs and gold for stars
Five 1/4-inch gold jingle bells
Green satin ribbon—two 8-inch lengths of 1/8-inch-wide ribbon for bows and one 9-inch length of 3/8-inch-wide ribbon for hanging loop

Additional Materials Needed (for reindeer stocking):
Felt—two 10-inch x 15-inch pieces of red for stocking; and one 9-inch x 12-inch piece or scraps each of dark green for cuff, medium blue for birds, brown for antlers, off-white for sack, tan for reindeer, black for hooves and gold for bird beaks and feet
Brown six-strand embroidery floss
2-inch square of white tissue paper
One 3/8-inch gold jingle bell
One 1/4-inch red pom-pom
Two 1/2-inch light green four-hole buttons

Green satin ribbon—one 8-inch length of 1/4-inch-wide ribbon for bow and one 9-inch length of 3/8-inch-wide ribbon for hanging loop

Finished Size: Each stocking measures about 9 inches wide x 14 inches long without hanging loop.

Directions:
STOCKING: Use photocopier to enlarge stocking and cuff patterns on next page to 200% or draw a 1-in. grid on tracing paper and trace the stocking and cuff patterns as shown onto the tracing paper with pencil.

For each stocking, place two pieces of red felt with wrong sides together and edges matching. Pin stocking pattern to felt. Cut out stocking, cutting through both layers of felt and pattern. Remove pattern.

For each stocking, cut out two cuff pieces from green felt as directed on pattern.

DOLL STOCKING APPLIQUES: Trace star pattern on next page and individual doll stocking patterns on page 68 onto tracing paper with pencil.

Cut out each shape from felt as directed on patterns.

Separate black six-strand embroidery floss and use two strands for backstitching and blanket stitching around shapes. See Fig. 1 for stitch illustrations.

Backstitch mouth on face and on large star where shown on patterns.

Use black dimensional paint to add two small dots to face and two larger dots to large star for eyes. Let dry.

Referring to patterns, stitch around all exposed edges of applique shapes with a small blanket stitch.

Referring to photo for placement, position star and doll applique shapes on front of one red stocking piece, overlapping shapes as shown on patterns. Glue appliques in place. Let dry.

Using black floss, hand-sew a jingle bell to each point of the large star.

Tie each length of 1/8-in.-wide green satin ribbon in a small bow. Glue a bow to each ponytail. Let dry.

Follow finishing instructions on next page to complete stocking.

REINDEER STOCKING APPLIQUES: Trace individual reindeer stocking patterns on page 68 onto tracing paper with pencil. Cut out each shape from felt as directed on patterns.

Separate black six-strand embroidery floss and use two strands for backstitching, straight stitching and blanket stitching around shapes. See Fig. 1 for stitch illustrations.

Trace "DEER FOOD" onto tissue paper. Pin traced pattern to front of sack. Backstitch over traced lettering, stitching through pattern and felt piece. Carefully remove tissue paper pattern.

Referring to patterns, stitch around exposed edges of all applique shapes except birds' beaks and feet with a small blanket stitch.

Using black floss, add a long straight stitch to each ear and backstitch mouth and eyebrows on the reindeer's head where shown on patterns.

Thread embroidery needle with unseparated brown floss and add three lazy daisy stitches to top of reindeer's head.

Use black dimensional paint to add two small dots to reindeer's head and a single black dot to each bird for eyes. Let dry.

Referring to photo for placement, use black floss to sew a button to the top of each reindeer leg.

Referring to photo for placement, position bird, sack and reindeer applique shapes on front of one red stocking piece, overlapping shapes as shown on patterns. Glue appliques in place. Let dry.

Tie the length of 1/4-in.-wide green satin ribbon in a small bow. Glue bow to neck of reindeer and gold jingle bell below ribbon. Let dry.

Glue pom-pom to reindeer's head for nose. Let dry.

Follow finishing instructions below to complete stocking.

FINISHING: For each stocking, pin two red felt stocking pieces with wrong sides together and edges matching.

Thread embroidery needle with unseparated black floss. Stitch around stocking through both layers of felt with a large blanket stitch, leaving top straight edge unstitched. See Fig. 1 for stitch illustration.

In same way, blanket-stitch along top and bottom edges of each green felt cuff piece separately.

Fold length of 3/8-in.-wide green satin ribbon in half for hanging loop.

Layer two cuff pieces with wrong sides together and edges matching. Slip the hanging loop between the cuff pieces along the left straight edge of the cuff. Pin as needed to hold.

Blanket-stitch the straight side edges of the cuff together, stitching through both layers and making sure to catch the ribbon hanging loop in the stitching on the left side.

Slip the cuff over the top of the stocking, lapping the wavy edge of the cuff over the top of the stocking as shown on the pattern. Glue bottom overlapped portion of cuff to front and back of stocking. Let dry.

Use red dimensional paint to add name to cuff of stocking. Let dry.

Hang with care this Christmas!

(More patterns on next page)

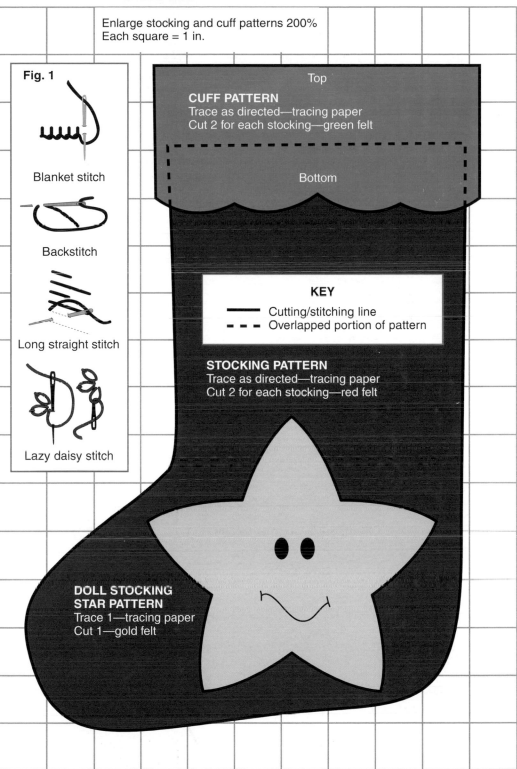

Enlarge stocking and cuff patterns 200%
Each square = 1 in.

Fig. 1

Blanket stitch

Backstitch

Long straight stitch

Lazy daisy stitch

Top

CUFF PATTERN
Trace as directed—tracing paper
Cut 2 for each stocking—green felt

Bottom

KEY
—— Cutting/stitching line
- - - Overlapped portion of pattern

STOCKING PATTERN
Trace as directed—tracing paper
Cut 2 for each stocking—red felt

DOLL STOCKING STAR PATTERN
Trace 1—tracing paper
Cut 1—gold felt

REINDEER STOCKING PATTERNS
Trace 1 each piece—tracing paper
Trace 1 each piece—color of felt indicated on pattern

DOLL STOCKING PATTERNS
Trace 1 each piece—tracing paper
Cut 1 each piece—color of felt
indicated on pattern

DEER
FOOD

Jolly St. Nick Has Real 'Kick'

COULD THIS sparkly little Santa pin *be* any cuter? Crafter Sandy Rollinger of Apollo, Pennsylvania creates her jolly old jingle-belling elf from wood, clay and beads.

"Pin him to your lapel and watch him kick up his heels for joy at the coming holidays," Sandy says with a laugh.

Materials Needed:

Pattern on this page
Tracing paper and pencil
3-inch square of 1/4-inch-thick smooth plywood
Scroll or band saw
Sandpaper
Tack cloth
Foam plate or palette
Paper towels
Water container
Acrylic craft paints—flesh, red and white
Small flat paintbrush
Blue dimensional fabric/craft paint
Oven-bake polymer clay—black, beige, red and white (Sandy used Sculpey III clay)
Waxed paper
Craft knife
Fine glitter—red and multicolored
White (tacky) glue
Jewelry findings—two 1-1/2-inch-long gold head pins and two 1-1/2-inch-long gold eye pins (found in jewelry section of craft stores)
4mm pony beads—six red and two white
1/2-inch gold liberty bell
1/4-inch white pom-pom
3-inch square of lightweight cotton fabric for back of pin
Straight pins
Needle-nose pliers
1-1/2-inch pin back
Ruler
Glue gun and glue sticks
Scissors

Finished Size: St. Nick pin measures about 1-7/8 inches wide x 3-1/8 inches high.

Directions:

Trace pattern at right onto tracing paper with pencil. Cut out shape on traced pattern lines.

Place pattern right side up on 3-in. square of wood with grain lines matching. Trace around shape with pencil. Cut out shape with scroll or band saw.

Sand wood to smooth and wipe with tack cloth.

Keep paper towels and a container of water handy to clean brushes. Place dabs of each paint color on foam plate or palette as needed. Add coats of paint as needed for complete coverage. Let paint dry after every application.

Refer to photo and pattern as a guide while painting as directed in the instructions that follow.

Paint entire wood piece white.

Turn pattern over and rub side of pencil lead over pattern lines to darken. Place pattern on painted wood piece with edges matching. Trace over inside pattern lines with dull pencil to transfer pattern onto wood.

Paint face flesh.

Paint suit and hat red, leaving bands of white where shown on pattern.

Apply white glue to red areas of wood piece. Liberally sprinkle fine red glitter over glue. When dry, shake off excess glitter. Repeat for white painted areas, sprinkling on multicolored glitter instead of red.

Knead each color of clay until soft and smooth, making sure to wash your hands each time you use a new color of clay. To prevent colors from mixing, work each color on a separate sheet of waxed paper. Use craft knife to cut clay pieces.

Roll a 1/2-in. ball of white clay into an 1/8-in.-thick rope. Cut the rope into eight 1/4-in.-long pieces. Press the pieces onto the front of St. Nick below the mouth for the beard. Cut a 3/4-in.-long piece of the white rope and press it above the beard for mustache.

Roll an 1/8-in. ball of beige clay for nose. Press nose onto center of the mustache.

Roll a 1/2-in. ball of red clay into a 1/4-in.-thick rope. Cut two 1/2-in.-long pieces for arms.

Roll two 1/4-in. balls of white clay. Press a ball onto one end of each arm, flattening each ball slightly for trim of suit.

Roll a 3/8-in. ball of beige clay for hands. Press trim of each arm onto opposite sides of clay hands.

Carefully press assembled arm piece onto front of St. Nick. Press top of liberty bell in place at bottom of clay hands. Remove bell.

Roll two 1/4-in. balls of black for boots. Flatten each into a small oval. Press a head pin into the top of each black boot.

Carefully remove clay pieces from St. Nick. Bake all clay pieces following man-ufacturer's directions. Let cool.

Use wire cutters to cut each eye pin to a 1-in. length. Referring to photo for placement, glue the eye pins to the back of St. Nick.

Pin St. Nick pattern right side up onto wrong side of fabric for back of pin. Cut out shape, cutting just inside traced pattern lines. Using white glue, glue fabric right side up onto back of St. Nick, covering straight ends of eye pins. Let dry.

Thread a white bead and then three red beads onto each head pin. Use needle-nose pliers to bend end of each head pin to make a loop at the top of the beads. Use wire cutters to cut away excess wire from head pin. Thread the loop of each head pin through the loop of an eye pin, making sure the toes of the boots face the front. Use needle-nose pliers to close loops.

Using glue gun, glue remaining clay pieces to front of St. Nick's body and liberty bell to hands as before. Glue pom-pom to tip of hat. Glue pin back centered on the back of St. Nick.

Add two small dots of blue dimensional paint to face for eyes. Let dry. Pin on a coat or favorite outfit! ✦

WOOD ST. NICK PIN PATTERN

Trace 1—tracing paper
Cut 1—1/4-in. plywood
Cut 1 as directed—fabric

Tree Skirt Rings Out a Merry Christmas Note

YULE START the holidays off on just the right note with this bright and easy tree skirt. Fashioned from felt by Sheryl Radakovich of Portage, Indiana, it features a heavenly host of adorable angels caroling the season's best to all your family and friends.

Materials Needed:
Patterns on next page
Tracing paper and pencil
Felt—44-inch square of red for tree skirt; three 9-inch x 12-inch pieces each of cream for wings, blue for dresses and black for hair and music notes; one 5-inch x 8-inch piece each of dark green for hearts and light peach or ivory for hands and faces; and one 4-inch square each of brown and tan for hair
4 yards of 1/2-inch-wide dark green braid trim
27-inch length of 1/4-inch-wide dark green satin ribbon
12-inch length of 1/8-inch gold metallic cord
Two skeins of black six-strand embroidery floss
Embroidery needle
Nine 5/8-inch light blue buttons
Black dimensional fabric/craft paint
Powdered cosmetic blush
Cotton swab
Quilter's marking pen or pencil
String
Yardstick or long ruler
White (tacky) glue
Standard sewing supplies

Finished Size: Tree skirt measures about 40 inches across.

Directions:
Fold red felt square in half to make a 22-in. x 44-in. piece. Fold piece in half crosswise to make a 22-in. square.

Tie string to quilter's marking pen or pencil about 1 in. above the tip. Measure and mark the string 20 in. from marking pen or pencil.

Referring to Fig. 1 below right, use one hand to hold the mark on the string to the folded point of the felt square. Holding the marking pen or pencil upright, use your other hand to draw an arc across the fabric.

Make another mark on the string 2 in. from marking pen or pencil. Hold this mark to the folded point of the felt square and draw an arc across the fabric as you did before.

Cut through all layers of felt on the marked lines. Unfold fabric for a 40-in.-diameter circle with a 4-in. opening in the center.

With yardstick or long ruler and quilter's marking pen or pencil, draw a line from center opening to outer edge of circle. Cut circle open along this line.

Leaving 1/2 in. of braid extending beyond each side of opening, glue green braid trim around edge of outer circle to opposite cut edge. Fold excess braid even with edge of opening and glue it to back of tree skirt. Glue green braid trim to edge of inner circle in the same way. Let dry.

Trace individual patterns at right onto tracing paper with pencil. Cut out and open folded patterns.

Cut out each shape from felt as directed on patterns.

Separate black six-strand embroidery floss and use two strands for all stitching. See Fig. 2 on next page for all stitch illustrations.

Backstitch eyelashes on each face.

Referring to patterns and photo, blanket-stitch around all exposed edges of all applique shapes except hearts and music notes, stitching a small blanket stitch around smaller shapes and a larger blanket stitch around larger shapes.

Referring to photo for placement, pin three hearts to the right side of each dress. Stitch hearts in place with long straight stitches.

Cut gold cord into three 4-in. lengths for halos. Glue the ends to the back of each angel's head, leaving cord free across the front. Let dry.

Referring to photo for placement, position angel applique shapes right side up on right side of tree skirt, overlapping shapes as shown on patterns and in photo. Glue appliques in place. Let dry.

Cut green satin ribbon into three 9-in. lengths. Tie each length into a small bow. Glue a bow to the neck of each angel's dress. Trim ends as desired. Let dry.

Referring to photo for placement, glue three buttons to the front of each angel's dress. Let dry.

Glue music notes to right side of tree skirt where desired. Let dry.

Use cotton swab and a circular motion to apply powdered blush to cheeks.

Use black dimensional paint to add a mouth to the face of each angel. Let dry.

Trim your tree from the bottom up with this choir of angels! ✿

Fig. 1 Cutting circle

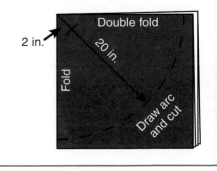

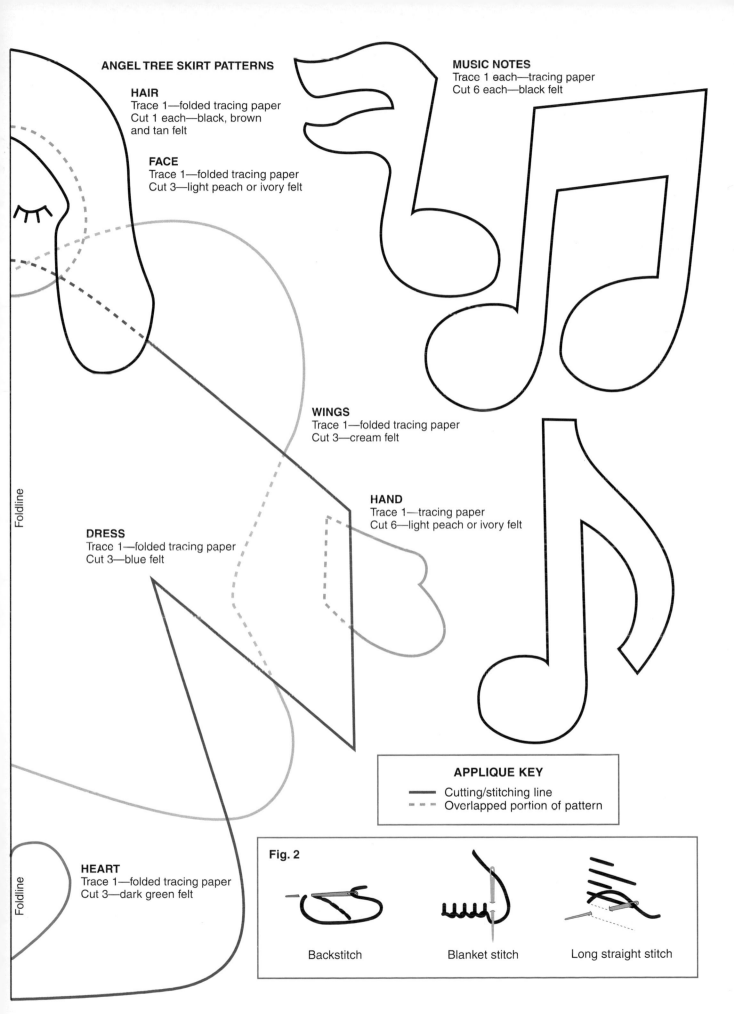

ANGEL TREE SKIRT PATTERNS

HAIR
Trace 1—folded tracing paper
Cut 1 each—black, brown
and tan felt

FACE
Trace 1—folded tracing paper
Cut 3—light peach or ivory felt

MUSIC NOTES
Trace 1 each—tracing paper
Cut 6 each—black felt

WINGS
Trace 1—folded tracing paper
Cut 3—cream felt

HAND
Trace 1—tracing paper
Cut 6—light peach or ivory felt

DRESS
Trace 1—folded tracing paper
Cut 3—blue felt

Foldline

HEART
Trace 1—folded tracing paper
Cut 3—dark green felt

Foldline

APPLIQUE KEY
——— Cutting/stitching line
- - - Overlapped portion of pattern

Fig. 2

Backstitch

Blanket stitch

Long straight stitch

Keep Season Bright with Cross-Stitched Kitchen Set

EVERGREENS, cardinals and bits of holly keep Yuletide memories right at your fingertips with this cross-stitched tea towel and pot holder set.

Designed by Westfield, New Jersey stitcher Lois Winston in soft shades of mauve and green, the handy duo makes a lovely and useful gift.

Materials Needed (for both):

Charts on this page and the next page
14-inch x 24-inch ecru fringed terry cloth towel with 3-inch-wide 14-count Aida cloth insert (Lois used a Charles Craft Kitchen Mates towel)
Quilted terry cloth pot holder with a 14-count Aida cloth pocket measuring 5 inches high x 7 inches across (Lois used a Charles Craft Kitchen Mates pot holder)
DMC six-strand embroidery floss in colors listed on color key
Size 24 tapestry needle
Scissors

Finished Size: Design area of towel is 35 stitches high x 161 stitches wide and measures about 2-1/2 inches high x 11-1/2 inches wide.

Design area of pot holder is 35 stitches high x 61 stitches wide and measures about 2-1/2 inches high x 4-1/4 inches wide.

Directions:

TOWEL: Fold Aida cloth insert of towel in half lengthwise and then in half crosswise to determine the center and mark this point.

To find center of towel chart, draw lines across chart, connecting opposite arrows. Begin stitching at this point so design will be centered.

Working with 18-in. lengths of six-strand floss, separate strands and use two strands for cross-stitches. See Fig. 1 (below right) for stitch illustration.

Each square on chart equals one stitch worked over a set of fabric threads. Use the colors indicated on the color key

to complete cross-stitching.

Do not knot floss on back of work. Instead, leave a tail of floss on back of work and hold it in place while working the first few stitches over it. To end a strand, run needle under a few neighboring stitches in back before cutting floss close to work.

POT HOLDER: Fold Aida cloth insert of pot holder in half lengthwise and then in half crosswise to determine center and mark this point.

Count from center to top row of pot holder chart. Locate the same position on Aida cloth insert. Begin stitching here for a centered design.

Stitch pot holder the same as for towel.

FINISHING: When stitching is complete, and only if necessary, gently wash stitched pieces in lukewarm water. Press each right side down on another terry towel to dry.

Then deck your kitchen with festive flair all winter long! ✪

COLOR KEY	DMC
☐ Very Light Antique Gold	834
■ Dark Beige Brown	839
■ Ultra Dark Pistachio Green	890
■ Very Dark Garnet	902
■ Medium Dark Antique Mauve	3726
■ Medium Light Antique Mauve	3727
☐ Dark Celadon Green	3815
■ Light Celadon Green	3817

POT HOLDER CHART

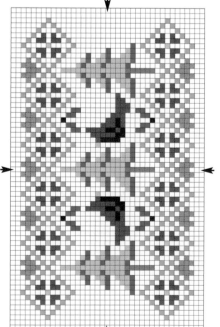

TEA TOWEL CHART

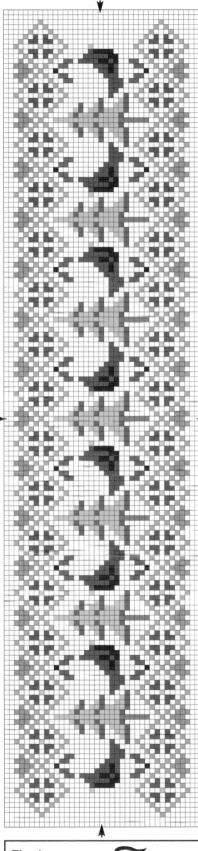

Fig. 1
Cross-stitch

This Scrappy Wrap's in the Bag

TRIM UP some novel gift wrap in a twinkling with this inexpensive idea from Lenora Schut of Pella, Iowa.

"It's a pretty and practical way to use up all the leftover ribbon we crafters keep around," Lenora says.

Materials Needed:
8-inch-wide x 10-inch-high brown paper gift bag
Parchment card stock—one 7-1/4-inch x 3-1/4-inch piece for gift bag trim and one 2-5/8-inch x 3-5/8-inch piece for gift tag
Red satin ribbon—9-inch length of 1/4-inch-wide ribbon and 12-inch length of 1/8 inch-wide ribbon
Ruler
Green fine-line permanent marker or gel pen
Scrap of yellow card stock or construction paper
Round paper punch
White (tacky) glue
Scissors

Finished Size: Excluding handles, gift bag measures about 8 inches wide x 10 inches high. Gift tag measures 1-3/4 inches wide x 2-5/8 inches high.

Directions:
GIFT BAG: Glue 7-1/4-in. x 3-1/4-in. piece of parchment card stock centered on front of gift bag about 2 in. from bottom of bag.

Cut a 2-in. length of 1/4-in.-wide ribbon. Cut one end of the ribbon piece at an angle as shown in photo. Glue ribbon to center of parchment card stock about 1/2 in. from bottom.

Cut two 1-3/4-in. lengths of 1/4-in.-wide ribbon. Cut one end of each ribbon piece at an angle. Glue a ribbon piece to card stock on opposite sides of

Trim Tip

HANDMADE trims can turn brown lunch bags into festive wraps. Let the children decorate bags with merry drawings and glitter glue designs. Or trace cookie cutter shapes onto construction paper to make trees, snowmen and gingerbread boys the kids can cut out, trim with crayons and craft scraps and then glue on.

center ribbon piece.

Cut three 1/4-in.-long teardrop shapes from yellow card stock or construction paper. To make flames for candles, glue a teardrop shape to the top of each ribbon piece. Use green marker or gel pen to draw pine boughs freehand around bottom of candles where shown in photo.

GIFT TAG: Fold 2-5/8-in. x 3-5/8-in. piece of parchment card stock in half crosswise to make a 1-3/4-in.-wide x 2-5/8-in.-high folded gift tag.

With fold at the left, use paper punch to make a hole through both layers in the upper left corner of the gift tag.

Cut a 1-3/4-in. length of 1/4-in.-wide ribbon. Cut one end of the ribbon piece at an angle. With fold at the left, glue ribbon to center front of gift tag about 3/4 in. from bottom.

Cut one 1/4-in.-long teardrop shape from yellow card stock or construction paper. Glue teardrop shape to the top of ribbon piece for flame of candle.

Use green marker or gel pen to draw pine boughs freehand around bottom of candle.

Thread 1/8-in.-wide ribbon through hole in gift tag. Tie gift tag to handle of gift bag—and it's all ready to hold a present for someone special! ✪

Cute Figures Cap Pencils With Cheer

THESE clever wood pencil toppers are sure to keep Christmas dreams—and lists—close at hand!

Designed by Sandy Rollinger of Apollo, Pennsylvania, the droll Santa and chubby cherub also can hold their own as tiny Yuletide shelf-sitters tucked all through the house.

"And they look so adorable peeking out of the top of the kids' stockings," Sandy notes.

Materials Needed (for both):
Patterns on this page
Tracing paper and pencil
Two 3-inch squares of 1-inch pine (1-inch pine is actually 3/4 inch thick)
Scroll or band saw
Drill with 5/16-inch bit or bit to match diameter of pencil
Sandpaper
Tack cloth
Foam plate or palette
Paper towels
Water container
Acrylic craft paints—black, light blue, light brown, pink, purple, white and red
Paintbrushes—1/4-inch flat, 1/2-inch flat, small round and liner
Toothpick
Textured snow medium
Craft foam—scraps each of white and yellow
White (tacky) glue
Clear acrylic sealer
Two standard-size pencils
Scissors

Finished Size: Angel pencil topper is about 2-3/4 inches wide x 2-1/8 inches tall. Santa pencil topper is about 1-3/4 inches wide x 2-1/8 inches tall.

Directions:
Trace angel and Santa patterns onto tracing paper with pencil. Cut out each, following outline of patterns.

Place a pattern on each wood piece with grain lines matching. Trace around patterns with pencil. Cut out each shape with scroll or band saw.

Drill a 3/4-in.-deep hole into the bottom of each shape where shown on the pattern.

Sand each shape smooth. Wipe with tack cloth to remove sanding dust.

Trace wing and halo patterns onto tracing paper. Cut out each shape. Use pencil to trace around wings onto white craft foam and around halo onto yellow craft foam. Cut out shapes, cutting just inside traced pattern lines.

PAINTING: Keep paper towels and a container of water handy to clean brushes. Place dabs of each paint color on foam plate or palette as needed. Add coats of paint as needed for complete coverage, extending paints onto sides and backs of each piece. Let paint dry after every application.

Refer to photo and patterns as guides while painting as directed in the instructions that follow.

Angel: Use 1/2-in. flat brush to paint entire shape white.

Turn angel pattern over and rub side of pencil lead over pattern lines to darken. Place pattern on cutout wood piece with edges matching. Trace over inside pattern lines with a dull pencil to transfer pattern onto wood.

Mix a small amount of white paint with pink to make light pink. Use 1/4-in. flat brush and mixed paint to paint face onto one side only.

Dip 1/4-in. flat brush into pink and wipe brush on paper towel to remove excess paint. With a nearly dry brush and a circular motion, add cheeks to face.

Use 1/4-in. flat brush and light brown to paint hair.

Use 1/2-in. flat brush and light blue to paint dress.

Use liner and purple to add horizontal and vertical lines to dress, spacing them about 1/4 in. apart. In the same way, add white horizontal and vertical lines to dress.

Use round brush and white to add dots around top and bottom of dress.

Dip toothpick into black and add two tiny dots for eyes.

Use liner and black to add mouth.

Apply sealer to angel following manufacturer's instructions.

Use liner and black to outline wings.

Glue the halo and the wings to the

WOOD PENCIL TOPPERS PATTERNS
Trace 1 each—tracing paper

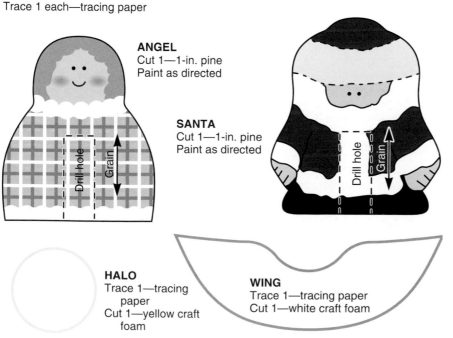

ANGEL
Cut 1—1-in. pine
Paint as directed

Drill hole · Grain

SANTA
Cut 1—1-in. pine
Paint as directed

Drill hole · Grain

HALO
Trace 1—tracing paper
Cut 1—yellow craft foam

WING
Trace 1—tracing paper
Cut 1—white craft foam

back of the angel. Let dry.

Santa: Use 1/2-in. flat brush to paint entire shape white.

Turn Santa pattern over and rub side of pencil lead over pattern lines to darken. Place pattern on cutout wood piece with edges matching. Trace over inside pattern lines with a dull pencil to transfer pattern onto wood.

Use 1/4-in. flat brush and black to paint boots.

Mix a small amount of white paint with pink to make a light pink. Use mixed paint to paint hands and face on one side only.

Mix white with a bit of light blue. Use 1/4-in. flat brush and mixed paint to paint hat trim.

Use liner and black to add two tiny dots to face for eyes and to add remaining details as shown.

Use 1/4-in. flat brush and red to paint jacket front and hat as shown on pattern. Paint entire jacket back red.

Use 1/4-in. flat brush to add textured snow medium to beard on front, hair on back and to jacket trim. Add a dollop of textured snow medium to top of hat. Let dry.

Apply sealer to Santa following manufacturer's instructions.

Place toppers on pencils and use them to stuff stockings this Christmas!

Pretty Pine-settia Is Abloom with Possibilities

PINING FOR a novel way to brighten your decor for Christmas? Clever crafter Jennie Chapman of Phoenix, Arizona uses pinecones and fabric to create this festive desktop "pine-settia".

Materials Needed:
Patterns on this page
Tracing paper and pencil
Lightweight cardboard
Glue stick
3mm chenille stems (pipe cleaners)—
   3 green and 16 red
1/8 yard each of green and red 44-inch-
   wide tissue lamé fabric
One large dry and opened pinecone
Scrap of yellow paper
1/4-inch round paper punch
White (tacky) glue
Glue gun and glue sticks
Wire cutters
Scissors

Finished Size: Pine-settia measures about 4 inches high x 8 inches across. Finished size will vary depending on size of pinecone used.

Directions:
Trace pattern below onto folded tracing paper with pencil. Cut out and open each for complete pattern.

Use glue stick to glue each pattern onto lightweight cardboard. Cut out each, following outline of pattern.

Use wire cutters to cut red chenille stems into the following pieces: Six 11-in. lengths for extra-large petals, six 10-in. lengths for large petals, four 6-in. lengths for medium petals and three 4-in. lengths for small petals. Bend each length of chenille stem in half.

Place 11-in. chenille stem over outline of extra-large leaf pattern with fold at pointed end of leaf. Shape chenille stem, following outline of pattern. Repeat to make six extra-large petals.

In the same way, shape remaining lengths of red chenille stems to make six large, five medium and four small petals.

Apply bead of white glue on one side of red petal-shaped chenille stem. Place chenille stem glue-side down onto wrong side of red tissue lamé fabric. Press chenille stem onto fabric until firmly glued. Repeat with each remaining red petal-shaped chenille stem, gluing each onto a new area of fabric. Let dry.

Use wire cutters to cut three 11-in. lengths of green chenille stem. Shape each as for red petals, following the outline of the extra-large petal pattern.

Following instructions for red petals, glue each shaped green chenille stem onto green tissue lamé fabric. Let dry.

Use scissors to cut out red and green petals, cutting along outside edge of chenille stems.

Starting at the base of the pinecone and using glue gun, glue straight end of petals to pinecone, placing the green and largest red petals near the bottom and adding smaller red petals toward the top as shown in the photo.

Punch circles from yellow paper with paper punch. Use white glue to adhere yellow circles to exposed tips of center of pinecone. Shape petals as desired.

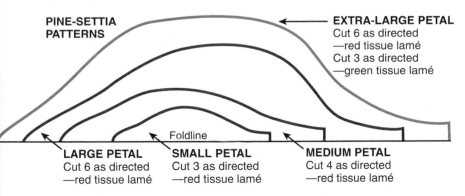

PINE-SETTIA PATTERNS

EXTRA-LARGE PETAL
Cut 6 as directed
—red tissue lamé
Cut 3 as directed
—green tissue lamé

Foldline

LARGE PETAL
Cut 6 as directed
—red tissue lamé

SMALL PETAL
Cut 3 as directed
—red tissue lamé

MEDIUM PETAL
Cut 4 as directed
—red tissue lamé

Chase Away Winter's Chill With This Natty Knitwear

BUNDLE UP your favorite boy in this sweater and let the winter winds blow!

Designed by Bridgetown, Nova Scotia crafter Susan Robicheau, this good-looking hefty pullover could warm the heart of Old Man Winter himself.

Materials Needed:
2-ply yarn—4(5,6,6) 4-ounce skeins with 215 yards per skein

of (BH) blue heather yarn and 3(3,4,4) 4-ounce skeins with 215 yards per skein of (W) off-white (Susan used 100% wool Briggs and Little Heritage yarns in Blue Heather and Washed White)
Knitting needles—size 5(3.75mm) and size 7(4.5mm) straight, and size 5(3.75mm) double pointed
Stitch holders
Yarn or tapestry needle
Scissors

Finished Size: Directions are for an Adult size Small sweater with a garment chest measurement of 40 inches. Changes for sizes Medium (44-inch chest), Large (48-inch chest) and Extra-Large (52-inch chest) are in parentheses.

Gauge:
Working in St st on size 7 needles, 18 sts and 24 rows = 4 inches.

Stitches Used:
STOCKINETTE STITCH: St st:
Row 1 (RS): Knit across row.
Row 2 (WS): Purl across row.
Repeat Rows 1 and 2.

Directions:
FRONT: Bottom Ribbing: Using smaller needles and BH, cast on 82(90,98,106) sts.
Row 1: * K 1, p 1; repeat from * across row: 82(90,98, 106) sts.
Repeat Row 1 until work measures 2(2,3,3) in., ending with a RS row.
Next Row: (WS): K 1, p across to last st, inc 6 sts evenly across row, k 1: 88(96,104,112) sts.
RIGHT FRONT: Blue heather section: Change to larger needles.
Row 1: (RS): K 2, [k 2, p 1, k 1] 10(11,12,13) times, k 1, inc 1, k 1, turn. Place remaining 44(48,52,56) sts on stitch holder: 45(49,53,57) sts on needle.
Row 2: K 1, p 2, [k 1, p 1, k 1, p 1] 10(11,12,13) times, k 2: 45(49,53,57) sts.

Row 3: K 2, [p 1, k 3] 10(11,12,13) times, p 1, k 2.
Row 4: K 1, p 1, k 1, [p 3, k 1] 10(11,12,13) times, p 1, k 1.
Row 5: K 1, p 1, [k 1, p 1, k 1, p 1] 10(11,12,13) times, k 1, p 1, k 1.
Row 6: K 1, p 2, [p 1, k 1, p 2] 10(11,12,13) times, p 1, k 1.
Row 7: K 2, [k 2, p 1, k 1] 10(11,12,13) times, k 3.
Rows 8-42: Repeat Rows 2-7 five more times, ending last repeat with Row 6: 45(49,53,57) sts.
Row 43: K across row: 45(49,53,57) sts. Do not fasten off.
Off-white and blue heather section: Attach W.
Row 1: (WS): K 1, p across row to last st, k 1: 45(49,53,57) sts.
Row 2: K across row.
Row 3: K 1W, p 2W, [p 1W, p 1BH, p 2W] 10(11,12,13) times, p 1W, k 1W.
Row 4: K 2W, [k 1W, k 1BH, k 1W, k 1BH] 10(11,12,13) times, k 3W.
Row 5: K 1W, p 1W, p 1BH, [p 3W, p 1BH] 10(11,12,13) times, p 1W, k 1W.
Row 6: Repeat Row 4.
Row 7: Repeat Row 3.
Row 8: With W, k across row.
Row 9: With W, k 1, p across row to last st, k 1: 45(49,53,57) sts. Fasten off BH.
Off-white section: Work with W only.
Row 1 (RS): K 2, [k 2, p 1, k 1] 10(11,12,13) times, k 3: 45(49,53,57) sts.
Row 2: K 1, p 2, [k 1, p 1, k 1, p 1] 10(11,12,13) times, p 1, k 1.
Row 3: K 2, [p 1, k 3] 10(11,12,13) times, p 1, k 2.
Row 4: K 1, p 2, [k 1, p 1, k 1, p 1] 10(11,12,13) times, p 1, k 1.
Rows 5-32: Repeat Rows 1-4 seven more times: 45(49,53,57) sts.
Row 33: Bind off 3(3,3,3) sts for armhole at beginning of row. Work in established pattern across row: 42(46,50,54) sts.
Row 34: Work across row in established pattern.
Row 35: K 1, sl 1, psso, work in established pattern across row: 41(45,49,53) sts.
Row 36: Repeat Row 34.
Row 37: Repeat Row 35: 40(44, 48,52) sts.
Row 38: Repeat Row 34.
Row 39: Repeat Row 35: 39(43, 47,51) sts.
Row 40: Repeat Row 34.
Row 41: Repeat Row 35: 38 (42,46,50) sts.
Row 42: Repeat Row 34.
Row 43: Repeat Row 35: 37(41, 45,49) sts.
Row 44: Repeat Row 34.

Continue to work even in established pattern until 37(39,43,45) rows above the beginning of the armhole have been worked: 37(41,45,49) sts.

Front neck shaping: Row 1: (RS): Bind off 14(16,18,20) sts at beginning of row. Work across row in established pattern to last 2 sts, k 2: 23(25,27,29) sts.

Row 2: K 1, work across row in established pattern to last 2 sts, p2tog: 22(24,26,28) sts.

Row 3: K2tog, work across row in established pattern to last 2 sts, k 2: 21(23,25,27) sts.

Rows 4-5: Repeat Rows 2 and 3:

Row 6: K 1, work across row in established pattern to last st, k 1: 19(21,23,25) sts.

Row 7: K 1, work across row in established pattern to last 2 sts, k 2.

Repeat Rows 6 and 7 until 48(54, 60,64) rows above the beginning of the armhole have been worked. Bind off remaining 19(21,23,25) sts.

LEFT FRONT: Off-white section: Using larger needles and W, attach yarn to WS of last row of bottom ribbing. Pick up 44(48,52,56) sts from stitch holder, k 1, inc 1, p across row to last st, k 1: 45(49,53,57) sts.

Row 1: (RS): K 2, [k 2, p 1, k 1] 10(11,12,13) times, k 3: 45(49,53,57) sts.

Row 2: K 1, p 2, [k 1, p 1, k 1, p 1] 10(11,12,13) times, p 1, k 1.

Row 3: K 2, [p 1, k 3] 10(11,12,13) times, p 1, k 2.

Row 4: K 1, p 2, [k 1, p 1, k 1, p 1] 10(11,12,13) times, p 1, k 1.

Rows 5-52: Repeat Rows 1-4 twelve more times: 45(49,53,57) sts. Fasten off W at end of Row 52.

Bottom blue heather section: Attach BH and k across row: 45(49,53,57) sts.

Row 1: (WS): K 1, p 2, [p 1, k 1, p 2] 10(11,12,13) times, p 1, k 1: 45(49,53,57) sts.

Row 2: K 2, [k 1, p 1, k 1, p 1] 10(11,12,13) times, k 3.

Row 3: K 1, p 1, k 1, [p 3, k 1] 10(11,12,13) times, p 1, k 1.

Row 4: K 2, [p 1, k 3] 10(11,12,13) times, p 1, k 2.

Row 5: K 2, p 1, [k 1, p 1, k 1, p 1] 10(11,12,13) times, k 2.

Row 6: K 2, [k 2, p 1, k 1] 10(11,12,13) times, k 3.

Rows 7-24: Repeat Rows 1-6 three more times: 45(49,53,57) sts. Do not fasten off.

Off-white and blue heather section: Attach W on WS row.

Rows 1-8: Repeat Rows 1-8 of the right front off-white and blue heather section: 45(49,53,57) sts.

Row 9: Bind off 3(3,3,3) sts at beginning of row, p across row to last st, k 1. Fasten off W: 42(46,50,54) sts.

Top blue heather section: Work with BH only.

Row 1: (RS): K 1, p 1, k 1, [k 2, p 1, k 1] 9(10,11,12) times, k 3: 42(46,50,54) sts.

Row 2: K 1, p 2, [k 1, p 1, k 1, p 1] 9(10,11,12) times, k2tog, k 1: 41(45,49,53) sts.

Row 3: K 2, [p 1, k 3] 9(10,11,12) times, p 1, k 3.

Row 4: K 2, [p 3, k 1] 9(10,11,12) times, k2tog, k 1: 40(44,48,52) sts.

Row 5: K 1, [k 1, p 1, k 1] 9(10,11,12) times, p 1, k 1.

Row 6: K 2, [k 2, p 1, k 1] 8(9,10,11) times, k 2, p 1, k2tog, k1: 39(43,47,51) sts.

Row 7: K 1, p 1, k 1, p 2, [p 2, k 1, p 2] 8(9,10,11) times, p 1, k 1.

Row 8: K 2, [k 1, p 1, k 1, p 1] 8(9,10,11) times, k 1, p 1, k2tog, k 1: 38(42,46,50) sts.

Row 9: K 1, p 1, k 1, p 1, k 1, [p 3, k 1] 8(9,10,11) times, p 2, k 1.

Row 10: K 2, p 1, k 3, [p 1, k 3] 8 (9,10,11) times, k2tog, k 1: 37(41,45,49) sts.

Row 11: K 1, p 1, [k 1, p 1, k 1, p 1] 8(9,10,11) times, p 1, k 1.

Row 12: K 2, [k 2, p 1, k 1] 8(9,10,11) times, k 3.

Continue to work even in established pattern until 36(38,42,44) rows above the beginning of the armhole have been completed, ending on a RS row: 37(41,45,49) sts.

Front neck shaping: Row 1: (WS): Bind off 14(16,18,20) sts at beginning of row. Work across row in established pattern to last 2 sts, p 1, k 1: 23(25,27,29) sts.

Row 2: K 2, work across row in established pattern to last 2 sts, k2tog: 22(24,26,28) sts.

Row 3: P2tog, work across row in established pattern to last 2 sts, p 1, k 1: 21(23,25,27) sts.

Rows 4-5: Repeat Rows 2 and 3.

Row 6: K 2, work across row in established pattern to last st, k 1: 19(21,23,25) sts.

Row 7: K 1, work across row in established pattern to last 2 sts, p 1, k 1.

Repeat Rows 6 and 7 until 48(54, 60,64) rows have been completed from the beginning of the armhole. Bind off remaining 19(21,23,25) sts.

BACK: Left Back: Work the same as for right front (eliminating neck shaping) until 48(54,60,64) rows from the beginning of the armhole have been completed. Bind off: 37(41,45,49) sts.

Right back: Work the same as for

left front (eliminating neck shaping) until 48(54,60,64) rows from the beginning of the armhole have been completed. Bind off: 37(41,45,49) sts.

SLEEVE (make 2): Cuff: Using smaller needles and BH, cast on 37(45,53,61) sts.

Row 1: (RS): K 1, * p 1, k 1; repeat from * across row.

Row 2: K 1, * k 1, p 1; repeat from * across to last st, k 1.

Repeat Rows 1 and 2 until work measures 2 in., ending with a WS row: 37(45,53,61) sts.

Sleeve: Change to larger needles.

Row 1: (RS): K 1, inc 1, k 1, [k 2, p 1, k 1] 8(10,12,14) times, k 2, inc 1, k 1: 39(47,55,63) sts.

Row 2: K 1, p 1, k 1, p 1, [k 1, p 1, k 1, p 1] 8(10,12,14) times, k 1, p 1, k 1.

Row 3: K 1, inc 1, k 2, [p 1, k 3] 8(10,12,14) times, p 1, k 2, inc 1, k 1: 41(49,57,65) sts.

Row 4: K 1, p 3, k 1, [p 3, k 1] 8(10,12,14) times, p 3, k 1.

Row 5: K 1, inc 1, p 1, k 1, p 1, [k 1, p 1, k 1, p 1] 8(10,12,14) times, [k 1, p 1,] twice, inc 1, k 1: 43(51,59,67) sts.

Row 6: [K 1, p 2] twice, [p 1, k 3] 8(10,12,14) times, p 1, k 1, p 2, k 1.

Row 7: K 3, p 1, k 1, [k 2, p 1, k 1] 8(10,12,14) times, [k 2, p 1] twice, k 3.

Row 8: [K 1, p 1] three times, [k 1, p 1, k 1, p 1] 8(10,12,14) times, [k 1, p 1] twice, k 1.

Row 9: K 1, p 1, k 3, [p 1, k 3] 8(10,12,14) times, p 1, k 3, p 1, k 1.

Row 10: K 2, p 3, k 1, [p 3, k 1] 8(10,12,14) times, p 3, k 2.

Row 11: K 1, inc 1, [k 1, p 1] twice, [k 1, p 1, k 1, p 1] 8(10,12,14) times, [k 1, p 1] twice, k 1, inc 1, k 1: 45(53,61,69) sts.

Row 12: K 1, p 3, k 1, p 2, [p 1, k 1, p 2] 8(10,12,14) times, p 1, k 1, p 3, k 1.

Row 13: K 4, p 1, k 1, [k 2, p 1, k 1] 8(10,12,14) times, k 2, p 1, k 4.

Row 14: K 2, [p 1, k 1] across row to last st, k 1.

Row 15: K 1, inc 1, k 1, p 1, k 3, [p 1, k 3] 8(10,12,14) times, p 1, k 3, p 1, k 1, inc 1, k 1: 47(55,63,71) sts.

Row 16: K 1, p 2, k 1, p 3, k 1, [p 3, k 1] 8(10,12,14) times, p 3, k 1, p 2, k 1.

Row 17: K 1, [k 1, p 1] across to last st, k 1.

Row 18: K 2, p 3, k 1, p 2, [p 1, k 1, p 2] 8(10,12,14) times, p 1, k 1, p 3, k 2: 47(55,63,71) sts. Do not fasten off BH.

Off-white and blue heather section: Row 1: (RS): With W, k across row: 47(55,63,71) sts.

Row 2: K 1, p across row to last st, k 1.

Row 3: [K 3W, k 1BH] across to last 3 sts, k 3W.

Row 4: K 1W, [p 1W, p 1BH] across *(Continued on next page)*

to last 2 sts, p 1W, k 1W.

Row 5: K 1W, inc 1W, [k 1BH, k 3W] 11(13,15,17) times, k 1BH, inc 1W, k 1W: 49(57,65,73) sts.

Row 6: K 1W, [p 1BH, p 1W] across to last st, k 1W.

Row 7: K 4W, k 1BH, [k 3W, k 1BH] 10(12,14,16) times, k 4W.

Row 8: With W, k 1, p across row to last st, k 1.

Row 9: With W, k 1, inc 1, k across row to last st, inc 1, k 1: 51(59,65,75) sts. Fasten off W.

Top blue heather section: Row 1: (WS): With BH, p across row: 51(59,65,75) sts.

Row 2: K 1, [p 1, k 3] 12(14,16,18) times, k 2.

Row 3: K 1, [p 1, k 1] across row.

Row 4: K 1, inc 1, k 2, [p 1, k 3] 11(13,15,17) times, p 1, k 2, inc 1, k 1: 53(61,67,77) sts.

Row 5: K 4, [p 1, k 3] across row to last st, k 1.

Row 6: K 1, [p 1, k 1] across row to last st, k 1.

Row 7: K 1, p 1, [k 1, p 3] 11(13,15,17) times, p 1, k 1.

Repeat Rows 2-7, working in established pattern while increasing at each end of every fourth row and incorporating pattern into increases until there are 85(95,107,117) sts on needle.

Work even until work measures 18(18-1/2,19,20) in. or desired sleeve length from the beginning, ending with a WS row.

Shoulder: Row 1: Bind off 3(3,5,5) sts at beginning of row, work across row in established pattern: 82(92, 102,112) sts.

Row 2: Bind off 3(3,5,5) sts at beginning of row, work across row in established pattern: 79(89,97,107) sts.

Row 3: K 1, sl 1, psso, work across row in established pattern to last 3 sts, k2tog, k 1: 77(87,95,105) sts.

Row 4: K 1, work across row in established pattern to last st, k 1.

Rows 5-10: Repeat Rows 3 and 4 three more times.

Bind off remaining 71(81,89,99) sts. With RS facing sew shoulder seams.

NECKBAND: Using smaller double-pointed needles, pick up and k 80(90,94,100) sts around neck opening.

Round 1: * K 1, p 1; repeat from * across: 80(90,94,100) sts.

Repeat Round 1 until work measures 2-1/2(2-1/2,3,3-1/2) in. Bind off. Fasten off, leaving 18 in. of yarn. Thread yarn or tapestry needle with tail of yarn. Fold neckband in half and sew bound-off edge to inside of sweater.

FINISHING: Use yarn or tapestry needle to sew top of sleeves to armhole of sweater body with RS facing.

With RS facing, sew side seams.

Use yarn or tapestry needle to weave in all loose ends.

Experienced knitters will enjoy brightening the holidays for some lad sure to appreciate this cozy gift idea! ⊕

ABBREVIATIONS	
inc	increase
k	knit
p	purl
psso	pass slipped stitch over
RS	right side
sl	slip
sts	stitch(es)
tog	together
WS	wrong side
* [ ]	Instructions following asterisk or between brackets are repeated as directed.

Trims to Make in a Twinkling

DURING this busy time of year, what do you do when visitors bearing gifts show up unexpectedly at your front door? Or unannounced guests stop by at dinnertime?

Why, welcome them in holiday style, of course!

It's easy with a snip of creativity and scraps on hand, says Carolyn Zimmerman from Fairbury, Illinois. She's an expert at whipping up quick crafts and trims to keep on hand for just such last-minute occasions.

"I use them as table favors or decorations—even as gifts," writes Carolyn, who explains in short order how to craft her nifty Soup-Can Snowman, Holly Berry Napkin Ring and Candy Cane Candle Holder.

"My Soup-Can Snowman (left) is a cinch for crafters of all ages," Carolyn promises. Simply cover a regular size soup can with white textured paint; then attach 1/4-in. black pompoms for eyes, nose and mouth, and twigs for arms. Add a piece of bright ribbon for a scarf, and a liquid soap lid sprayed black and trimmed with holly for a hat.

Puzzle pieces spray-painted green, glued together to form a circle and trimmed with mini red pompoms and a ribbon bow, are all it takes to make her Holly Berry Napkin Rings.

And finally, dress up plain red or green tapers with a holder made of six

candy canes turned upside down and tied securely with red and green ribbon. "A spot of hot glue on each cane makes them more secure," Carolyn adds, along with best wishes for your merry last-minute celebrations! ⊕

Her Spoonful of Nostalgia Adds Tasty Yuletide Touch

DISH UP a taste of Christmas past with this old-fashioned Santa ornament from crafter Lydia Hays of Wichita, Kansas.

Beginning with an old tablespoon, Lydia adds antique colors and bits of homespun fabric to fashion her unique tree trim. "But this Santa could also be a keepsake party favor for guests at holiday dinners or cookie exchanges," Lydia offers.

Materials Needed:
Pattern at lower right
Tracing paper and pencil
Dry ballpoint pen or stylus
Graphite paper
Old tablespoon
Rubbing alcohol and cotton ball
Foam plate or palette
Paper towels
Water container
Glass/metal conditioner (Lydia used FolkArt Glass and Tile Medium available at most craft stores)
Acrylic craft paints—Black, Cranberry Wine, Light Buttermilk, White, Mocha, Raspberry, Santa Flesh and Toffee (Lydia used DecoArt Americana paints)
Paintbrushes—1/2-inch flat, 1/4-inch angular, 6/0 liner, small scruffy brush and 1 inch foam brush
Toothpick
Painter's finishing wax or matte acrylic spray sealer
3/4-inch x 2-1/2-inch piece of 100% natural cotton quilt batting
Torn fabric strips—one 1-inch x 8-inch piece of cranberry-and-tan stripe for hanging loop and one 1-inch x 4-inch piece of dark green-and-cranberry plaid for trim
Tacky (white) glue
Scissors
6-inch length of 1/4-inch wooden dowel
Clamp (optional)

Finished Size: Spoon ornament is about 2 inches wide x 5-1/2 inches long without hanger. Finished size may vary depending on size of spoon used.

Directions:
Clamp or hold spoon to a sturdy surface and bend about 2 in. of handle around wooden dowel toward back of spoon.

Wash and dry spoon. Use cotton ball to wipe the back of the spoon with rubbing alcohol.

PAINTING: Keep paper towel and a basin of water handy to clean brushes. Place dabs of each paint color onto foam plate or palette as needed. Add coats of paint as needed to back of spoon for complete coverage. Let dry after every application.

Refer to photo and painting diagram as guides while painting as directed in the instructions that follow.

Following manufacturer's instructions, apply glass/metal conditioner to back of spoon with foam brush.

Use 1/2-in. flat brush and Cranberry Wine to paint top 1 in. for hat.

Use 1/2-in. flat brush and Light Buttermilk to paint bottom of spoon for face.

Trace face pattern onto tracing paper with pencil. Place pattern on back of spoon and slip graphite paper between pattern and spoon. Trace over lines of pattern with dry ballpoint pen or stylus to transfer pattern onto spoon.

Use 1/4-in. angular brush and Santa Flesh to paint face.

Dip the 1/4-in. angular brush into clean water. Touch the brush to a paper towel until brush is wet but not dripping.

Dip longer corner of brush into Toffee, then stroke the brush on a clean area of the foam plate or palette to blend paint and water. The color should fade from dark to light to clear. Pull the paint-filled edge along the edge of the mustache to shade.

Dip scruffy brush into Raspberry and remove excess on a paper towel. With a nearly dry brush and a circular motion, add cheeks. If needed, use 1/4-in. angular brush and Light Buttermilk to touch-up mustache.

Dip toothpick into Black and use to dab on two small ovals for eyes.

Dip toothpick into White and use to add a tiny highlight to top of each eye. Use liner and White to add a line to each to highlight.

Dip end of smallest paintbrush handle into Mocha and use to add a small dot for nose.

Dip toothpick into Mocha and use to add several small dots in groups of three to hat.

Apply finishing wax or spray sealer following manufacturer's instructions.

Fold strip of cotton batting in half lengthwise and glue to hold. Glue folded strip around spoon above eyes, wrapping ends to back. Trim excess.

Thread the cranberry-and-tan stripe fabric strip through loop of spoon handle. Tie ends of strip together in an overhand knot for hanging loop.

Wrap the dark green-and-cranberry plaid fabric around spoon handle and tie in an overhand knot above hat. Spot-glue as needed to hold. Hang on the tree for all to enjoy! 🔩

FACE PATTERN
Trace 1—tracing paper
Paint as directed in instructions

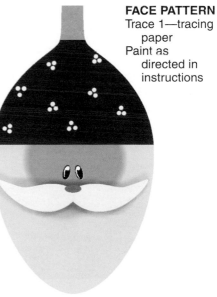

posite sides of a 4-1/2-in. red star print square as shown in Fig. 3. Repeat to make a total of four.

Lay out pieced sections in three rows as shown in Fig. 4. Sew rows together, carefully matching corners, to make an 8-1/2-in. square star block.

Repeat to make a total of four star blocks.

Nine-patch block (make 1): For the center nine-patch block, sew a 2-1/2-in. gold square to each short end of a 2-1/2-in. x 4-1/2-in. cream rectangle to make top row. Repeat for bottom row.

Sew a 2-1/2-in. x 4-1/2-in. cream rec-

Fig. 2a Making right unit (make 8)

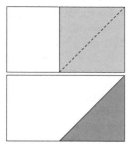

Fig. 3 Joining units

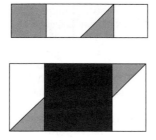

Fig. 5 Nine-patch assembly (make 1)

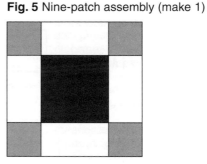

Fig. 2b Making left unit (make 8)

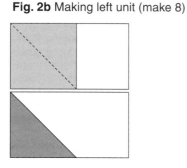

Fig. 4 Star block assembly (make 4)

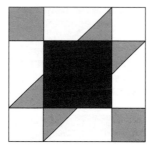

ASSEMBLY DIAGRAM

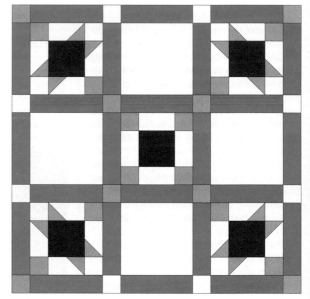

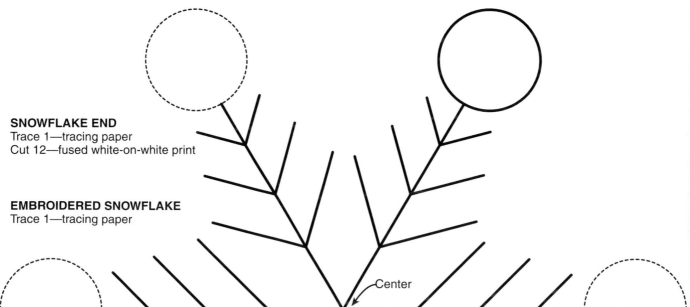

SNOWFLAKE END
Trace 1—tracing paper
Cut 12—fused white-on-white print

EMBROIDERED SNOWFLAKE
Trace 1—tracing paper

Center

Trace, flop and repeat for complete pattern

tangle to opposite sides of the remaining red star print 4-1/2-in. square.

Referring to Fig. 5, lay out the rows and assemble the nine-patch block as shown.

Assembly: Lay out the completed blocks, cornerstone squares and sashing strips as shown in the Assembly Diagram at left and photo on page 80, keeping stripes in sashings in the same direction.

Sew each row together as planned. Press seams in each row in opposite directions. Sew the rows together as planned, carefully matching corners. Press seams toward narrow sashing rows.

QUILTING: With wrong side up, smooth out the backing fabric on a flat surface. Center the batting on top. Center the pieced top on the batting with the right side up. Pin or hand-baste the layers together.

Using matching thread, machine-stitch in-the-ditch of all seams. Stitch around each snowflake and feather tree as shown in photo. If desired, machine-stitch a bow in the center nine-patch block with red thread.

Baste around pieced top a scant 1/4 in. from edges. Trim excess batting and backing even with pieced top.

HANGING SLEEVE: On each 4-in. x 16-in. hanging sleeve, turn 1/4 in. to the wrong side twice on each short end. With matching thread, sew close to first fold to hem.

Fold each piece in half lengthwise with wrong sides together. Pin each piece along top back edge of wall hanging with raw edges matching, leaving 1 in. between the pieces at the center.

With matching thread, hand-sew the fold of each hanging sleeve to backing.

BINDING: Join short ends of binding strips together with diagonal seams to make one long binding strip. Trim one short end of binding strip diagonally. Press trimmed end 1/4 in. to wrong side. Press strip in half lengthwise with wrong sides together.

Stitch binding to front of wall hanging with raw edges matching and a 1/4-in. seam, mitering corners and overlapping the ends. Trim excess binding.

Fold binding to back of wall hanging, encasing raw edges and mitering corners. Hand-sew fold of binding to backing, covering stitching.

FINISHING: Remove basting. Insert wooden dowel in hanging sleeve.

Cute Canister Drums Up Fun

LOOKING FOR a special container to package Yuletide presents from your pantry? You can't beat this thrifty gift canister designed by Mary Cosgrove of Rockville, Connecticut.

"It's a great way to recycle Christmas cards," Mary notes, "and it makes a cheery wrap for a teacher's gift."

Materials Needed:
Pattern on this page
Tracing paper and pencil
Empty 5-inch-high x 5-inch-diameter round container with plastic lid (Mary used a Poppycock Caramel Popcorn container)
Four old Christmas cards
Coordinating wrapping paper with a small print (Mary used red-and-white polka dot wrapping paper)
4-1/2 yards of 1/8-inch gold metallic cord
Four 3/4-inch brown buttons
Two red pony beads
Two round standard-size pencils for drumsticks
White (tacky) glue
Ruler
Scissors

Finished Size: Drum measures 5 inches across x 5 inches high. Drumsticks are 7-1/2 inches long.

Directions:
Trace triangle pattern onto tracing paper with pencil. Cut out eight triangles from wrapping paper.

Trim front of each Christmas card to a 4-in.-wide x 4-3/4-in.-high rectangle with design centered.

Glue Christmas card cutouts right side out to outside of canister with side edges touching.

Glue eight wrapping-paper triangles around top and bottom of container with points touching and leaving card designs exposed as shown in the photo.

Glue gold metallic cord to inside edges of triangles. Trim excess.

Glue a button over each intersection of gold cords.

Glue a pony bead to opposite sides of top of container.

Cut two 1-yard lengths of gold metallic cord. Thread one end of each length of cord through a pony bead. Tie ends of all cords together in an overhand knot. Trim ends as desired.

Cut two 1-1/4-in. x 6-3/4-in. pieces of wrapping paper. Glue wrapping paper around each pencil to cover.

Place pencil drumsticks in an "X". Wrap drumsticks with remaining gold cord and tie ends in a bow; trim ends as desired. Fill canister with cookies, candy or other treats!

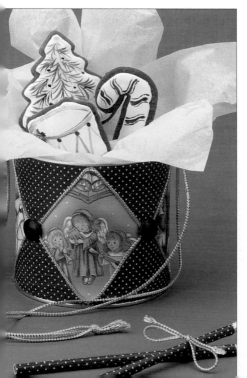

TRIANGLE PATTERN
Trace 1—tracing paper
Cut 8—wrapping paper

Noel Napkin Holder Keeps Holiday Memories Handy

CHRISTMAS MEMORIES are often wrapped around small family knick-knacks brought out each year to make the season merry. This tree-trimmed napkin holder from Cindy Groom-Harry of Ireton, Iowa is one of those.

"With a little help from an adult," Cindy suggests, "youngsters could glue the precut wood pieces together for a festive family-keepsake project."

Materials Needed:
1/16-inch-thick purchased wooden shapes—five 3/8-inch circles, four 2-1/2-inch squares, three 1-7/8-inch x 3-1/2-inch triangles, two 1-3/8-inch x 2-5/8-inch triangles and one 2-inch star (Cindy used Woodsies and Jumbo Woodsies)
1/16-inch-thick purchased wooden cutouts—three 3/8-inch-long candy canes and six 3/4-inch-long lightbulbs (Cindy used Woodsies Christmas I and Woodsies Christmas II cutouts)
Drill with 1/16-inch bit
1/4-inch wooden dowel—one 3-inch length and one 5-inch length
Finishing sandpaper
Paper towels
Water container
Foam plate or palette
Acrylic craft paints (Cindy used DecoArt Americana and Dazzling Metallics paints)—Avocado, Berry Red,
Glorious Gold, Light Cinnamon, Primary Yellow, Sapphire Blue, Shimmering Silver and Titanium White
Paintbrushes—small flat, small round and 1-inch foam brush
Brown spray stain (Cindy used Design Master Home Hickory Decor Spray Stain)
24-inch length of 24-gauge gold craft wire (Cindy used Artistic Wire/ Permanent Colored Wire)
2-1/2-inch x 5-inch piece of brown felt
Ruler
Needle-nose pliers
Newspapers
Glue gun and glue sticks (Cindy used an Adhesive Tech Ultimate Glue Gun and sticks)
Scissors

Finished Size: Wood napkin holder measures 5 inches across x 6 inches tall x 2 inches wide.

Directions:
Drill a hole through the base of each wooden lightbulb piece.

Lightly sand ends of dowel pieces and remaining wood pieces to smooth. Wipe with damp paper towel to remove sanding dust.

PAINTING: Keep paper towels and a container of water handy to clean brushes. Place dabs of paint on foam plate or palette as needed. Paint all

sides of wood pieces as directed. Add coats of paint as needed for complete coverage. Let paint dry after every application.

Referring to photo, paint as directed in the instructions that follow.

Use foam brush and Light Cinnamon to paint dowels and squares.

Use foam brush and Avocado to paint triangles.

Use foam brush and Glorious Gold to paint star.

Use flat brush and Sapphire Blue to paint two circles and two lightbulbs.

Use flat brush and Berry Red to paint one circle and two lightbulbs.

Use flat brush and Primary Yellow to paint two circles and two lightbulbs.

Use flat brush to paint three candy canes Titanium White.

Use round brush and Berry Red to add narrow diagonal stripes to one side of each candy cane.

Use round brush and Shimmering Silver to paint the base of each lightbulb.

Use liner and Titanium White to add a highlight to each bulb.

ASSEMBLY: Tree: Referring to photo, overlap and glue three larger triangles at different angles and add remaining two smaller triangles to the top.

Glue base of star to back of treetop.

Thread lightbulbs onto length of gold craft wire. Use needle-nose pliers to coil about 1-1/2 in. of wire at each end. Space lightbulbs along wire as desired and wrap wire between bulbs around pencil to coil. Glue lightbulbs to front of tree where desired.

Glue circles and candy canes to front of tree where desired.

Napkin holder: For base of napkin holder, place two squares on a flat surface. Glue side edges of squares together to make a 2-1/2-in. x 5-in. base.

In the same way, glue two more squares together to make a 2-1/2-in. x 5-in. back piece.

Stand back piece on its edge and glue long edge of base and back piece together with ends matching. Glue the 5-in. length of dowel along inner edge of glued pieces to stabilize.

Glue bottom edge of back of tree to front edge of base. Glue the 3-in. length of dowel along inner edge of back of tree to stabilize.

FINISHING: Place assembled napkin holder on a newspaper-covered surface.

Spray sides of tree, star and napkin holder base with brown stain. Spatter front of tree by partially depressing nozzle of spray stain. Let dry.

Glue felt to bottom of napkin holder base. Use scissors to trim felt even with edges of base. ✤

She'll Cozy Up to Christmas With Pretty Crocheted Set

NO MATTER how frightful the weather, this comforting set from Beverly Mewhorter of Apache Junction, Arizona will warm up the holidays!

Materials Needed (for all):
Two 5-ounce skeins of textured worsted-weight yarn (Beverly used Bernat Soft Boucle yarn in Medium Rose)
Size H/8 (5mm) crochet hook or size needed to obtain correct gauge
3-inch square of cardboard
Yarn or tapestry needle
Scissors

Gauge: 4 scs and 3 rows = 1 inch.

Finished Size: Scarf is 8 inches wide x 60 inches long without fringe. Adult size hat has a 22-inch circumference. Adult size mittens are 9 inches long and 8-1/2 inches around the hand.

Directions:
SCARF: Row 1: Ch 27, work 1 sc in second ch from hk and in each remaining ch across, turn: 26 scs.

Row 2: Ch 3 for first dc, dc in next sc, * ch 2, sk next 2 scs, dc in each of next 2 scs; repeat from * across, turn: 14 dcs and 6 ch-2 sps.

Row 3: Ch 3 for first dc, dc in next dc, * ch 2, sk next 2 chs, dc in next 2 dcs; repeat from * across, ending with a dc in third ch of beginning ch-3, turn: 14 dcs and 6 ch-2 sps.

Rows 4-82: Repeat Row 3: 14 dcs and 6 ch-2 sps.

Row 83: Ch 1 for first sc, sc in each dc and in each ch across: 26 scs. Fasten off.

Use yarn or tapestry needle to weave in all loose ends.

Fringe: Cut two 6-in.-long pieces of yarn. Working with two strands as one, fold yarn in half. Insert crochet hk into first sc of one narrow end of scarf. Draw fold of yarn through st to make a lp. Bring yarn ends through lp and pull ends to tighten lp around yarn.

In the same way, add yarn fringe to each sc at both ends of the scarf. Trim yarn ends even.

HAT: Round 1: Ch 4 for first dc, work 11 dcs in fourth ch from hk, join with a sl st in third ch of beginning ch-4: 12 dcs.

Round 2: Ch 3 (counts as first dc here and throughout), work 1 dc in same

st, work 2 dcs in each remaining dc around, join with a sl st in third ch of beginning ch-3: 24 dcs.

Round 3: Ch 3, work 1 dc in same st, work 2 dcs in each remaining st around, join with a sl st in third ch of beginning ch-3: 48 dcs.

Round 4: Ch 3, dc in same st, dc in next st, * work 2 dcs in next st, dc in next st; repeat from * around to last four sts, work 2 dcs in each of last four sts, join with a sl st in third ch of beginning ch-3: 74 dcs.

Round 5: Ch 3, dc in same st, * ch 2, sk next 2 dcs, dc in each of next 2 dcs; repeat from * around, ch 2, join with a sl st in third ch of beginning ch-3: 38 dcs and 19 ch-2 sps.

Rounds 6-11: Ch 3, dc in next dc, * ch 2, sk next 2 chs, dc in each of next 2 dcs; repeat from * around, ch 2, join with a sl st in third ch of beginning ch-3: 38 dcs and 19 ch-2 sps.

Round 12: Ch 3, dc in next dc, dc in each of next 2 chs, * dc in each of next 2 dcs, dc in each of next 2 chs; repeat from * around, join with a sl st in third ch of beginning ch-3: 76 dcs.

Round 13: Ch 1, sl st in each st around, join with a sl st in first st. Fasten off.

Use yarn or tapestry needle to weave in all loose ends.

Pom-pom: Wind matching yarn around 3-in. square of cardboard 40 times. Cut yarn at opposite edges of cardboard to make yarn pieces 3 in. long. Carefully remove cardboard. Tie another piece of yarn tightly around center of yarn pieces. Holding ends of tie, shake the pom-pom to fluff.

Thread long yarn ends onto yarn or tapestry needle and sew pom-pom to center top of hat. Fasten off. Trim ends as needed.

MITTENS (make two): Round 1: Ch 4 for first dc, work 11 dcs in fourth ch from hk, join with a sl st in third ch of beginning ch-4: 12 dcs.

Round 2: Ch 3 (counts as first dc here and throughout), work 1 dc in same st, work 2 dcs in each remaining dc around, join with a sl st in third ch of beginning ch-3: 24 dcs.

Rounds 3-8: Ch 3, dc in each remaining dc around, join with a sl st in third ch of beginning ch-3: 24 dcs.

Round 9: Ch 3, dc in next dc, ch 4,

sk 4 dcs for thumb opening, dc in each remaining dc around: 20 dcs.

Round 10: Ch 3, dc in each dc and in each ch around, join with a sl st in third ch of beginning ch-3: 24 dcs.

Rounds 11-13: Ch 3, dc in each dc around, join with a sl st in third ch of beginning ch-3: 24 dcs.

Round 14: Ch 1, sl st in each dc around, join with a sl st in first st. Fasten off.

Thumb: Round 1: With matching yarn, ch 4 for first dc, work 7 dcs in fourth ch from hk, join with a sl st in third ch of beginning ch-3: 8 dcs.

Rounds 2-4: Ch 3 for first dc, dc in each remaining dc around, join with a sl st in third ch of beginning ch-3: 8 dcs. Fasten off at end of Round 4.

Use yarn or tapestry needle and matching yarn to sew edge of Round 4 of thumb to thumb opening on mitten.

Use yarn or tapestry needle to weave in all loose ends. ✦

ABBREVIATIONS

ch(s)	chain(s)
dc(s)	double crochet(s)
hk	hook
lp	loop
sc(s)	single crochet(s)
sl st	slip stitch
sk	skip
sp(s)	space(s)
st(s)	stitch(es)
*	Instructions following asterisk are repeated as directed.

Jolly Santa Ho-Ho-Holds A Cupful of Good Wishes!

CHOCK-FULL of Christmas cheer, this jolly Santa treat cup makes a welcoming table favor for holiday dinner guests. "It goes together in no time and costs only pennies," says crafter Darlene Prazinak of Matlock, Manitoba.

With a little adult help, this could be a great Scout troop project to brighten trays for hospital patients or shut-ins.

Materials Needed:
Patterns on this page
Tracing paper and pencil

Ballpoint pen
8-inch x 11-inch piece of lightweight cardboard
Glue stick
Craft foam—scraps each of black, flesh, red and white
1-inch white pom-pom
7-ounce green paper cup
Powdered cosmetic blush
Cotton swab
Black and white acrylic craft paint
Small round paintbrush
Black fine-line permanent marker that will write on craft foam

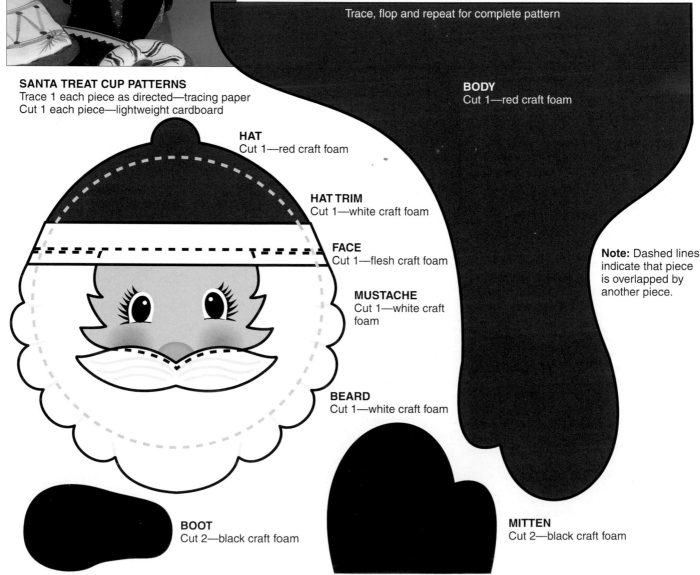

SANTA TREAT CUP PATTERNS
Trace 1 each piece as directed—tracing paper
Cut 1 each piece—lightweight cardboard

Trace, flop and repeat for complete pattern

BODY
Cut 1—red craft foam

HAT
Cut 1—red craft foam

HAT TRIM
Cut 1—white craft foam

FACE
Cut 1—flesh craft foam

MUSTACHE
Cut 1—white craft foam

BEARD
Cut 1—white craft foam

Note: Dashed lines indicate that piece is overlapped by another piece.

BOOT
Cut 2—black craft foam

MITTEN
Cut 2—black craft foam

White gel pen or white fine-line paint marker (optional)
White (tacky) glue
Scissors
Treats to fill cup

Finished Size: Santa treat cup is about 3 inches wide x 7 inches high.

Directions:

Use pencil to trace individual pattern pieces on previous page onto tracing paper as directed on patterns.

Use glue stick to glue patterns onto lightweight cardboard.

Cut out each shape on traced lines of pattern for templates.

Use ballpoint pen to trace around templates onto color of craft foam indicated on patterns.

Cut out each shape, cutting just inside traced lines.

Use pencil to add detail lines on beard and mustache as shown on the patterns.

Refer to patterns and photo at far left as a guide for all painting and gluing. Use white (tacky) glue for all gluing.

Use round brush to paint white eyes on Santa's face. Let dry.

Use round brush and black to add a pupil to each eye. Let dry.

Dip round brush into white and use to add a tiny dot to each eye for highlight. Let dry.

Use black marker to add eyelashes.

Use cotton swab and a circular motion to apply powdered blush to Santa's cheeks and nose.

With edges matching, glue a black mitten to right side of each hand on body. Let dry.

With black mittens on outside and straight edge aligned with bottom of paper cup, wrap and glue body around outside of paper cup.

Overlap and glue mittens in front as shown in photo at left. Glue boots to the cup just below mittens. Let dry.

To add snowflakes to rest of paper cup, add white dots and tiny plus signs with a line through each to exposed areas of paper cup. Let dry.

Glue beard and hat to face with straight edges meeting as shown on pattern. Let dry.

Glue hat trim centered along bottom of hat as shown on pattern.

Glue Santa's mustache right side up onto the right side of beard.

Glue assembled face to body piece, making sure bottom of beard overlaps rim of cup. Let dry.

Glue pom-pom to top of hat. Let dry.

Fill cup with tasty holiday treats and celebrate the season! ⊕

Frosty Pins Down Warm Smiles

MUFFLED IN Christmas colors, this funny, frosty fellow will break the ice and kindle warm smiles wherever you wear him.

Designer Helen Rafson of Louisville, Kentucky describes her perky little pin as quick and easy, adding, "If you can make a snowball, you can make this snowman!"

Materials Needed:
Pattern on this page
Tracing paper and pencil
Two 3-inch squares of white felt
Straight pins
Six-strand embroidery floss—black and white
Embroidery needle
Polyester stuffing
Powdered cosmetic blush
Cotton swab
Two 4mm black seed beads
Two 1/4-inch green pom-poms
Two small black snaps
7-inch length of red yarn for scarf
1-1/2-inch length of black florist wire
Seam sealant (optional)
1-1/2-inch pin back
White (tacky) glue

Finished Size: Snowman pin measures about 2 inches across x 2-3/8 inches high.

Directions:
Trace snowman pattern onto tracing paper with pencil.

Layer white felt pieces with wrong sides together and edges matching. Pin snowman pattern to layered felt. Cut out shape, cutting through both layers of felt and pattern. Remove pattern.

Separate black six-strand embroidery floss and thread embroidery needle with two strands. Referring to pattern for placement, stitch mouth on one felt snowman piece with a short running stitch. See Fig. 1 for stitch illustrations.

Using two strands of black embroidery floss, sew black beads close together above mouth for eyes.

Use cotton swab and a circular motion to apply powdered blush to cheeks.

Separate white six-strand floss and thread embroidery needle with three strands. Place both felt snowman pieces with wrong sides together and edges matching. Sew around outer edges of body with a small blanket stitch, inserting stuffing between the layers as you sew. See Fig. 1 for stitch illustrations.

Wrap red yarn around neck of snowman and tie ends in a knot at one side. Apply seam sealant to the yarn ends if desired.

Bend black florist wire piece into a half circle. Glue ends of wire to opposite sides of snowman's head. Let dry.

Glue a green pom-pom over each end of wire for earmuffs. Let dry.

Glue snaps to front of snowman. Let dry.

Glue pin back across back of snowman. Let dry.

Enhance your wintry wardrobe with this cute character! ⊕

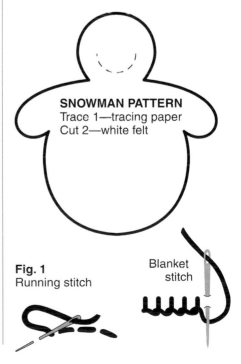

SNOWMAN PATTERN
Trace 1—tracing paper
Cut 2—white felt

Fig. 1
Running stitch

Blanket stitch

Light Up the Season with Cozy Sweatshirt

BRIGHT BULBS and a whimsical Christmas tree spruce up this everyday sweatshirt in such happy holiday style! Donna Stefanik of Westfield, Massachusetts supplies easy-to-follow directions for her applique design here.

Materials Needed:
Patterns on this page
Pencil
Red cotton/polyester blend sweatshirt
100% cotton or cotton-blend fabrics—
    5-inch x 8-inch piece of green Christmas print for tree (Donna used a novelty print with candy cane, star and tree shapes); 6-inch square of small gold print for lightbulb bases; and scraps each of small blue, green, orange, purple, red, white and yellow prints for lightbulbs
1/4 yard of paper-backed fusible web
5/8-inch gold metallic star-shaped button
Black six-strand embroidery floss or black pearl cotton
Embroidery needle
Quilter's marking pen or pencil (optional)
Black permanent fabric marker or black

dimensional fabric/craft paint
Standard sewing supplies

Finished Size: Design measures about 7-1/2 inches wide x 9 inches high and is shown on a Child size Medium sweatshirt.

Directions:
Hand-wash all fabrics without fabric softeners, washing colors separately. If the water from any fabric is discolored, wash again until rinse water runs clear. Dry and press all fabrics.

Wash and dry sweatshirt following manufacturer's instructions.

Trace patterns onto paper side of fusible web as directed on patterns, leaving 1/2 in. between shapes. Cut shapes apart, leaving a margin of paper around each.

Fuse shapes onto wrong side of fabrics as directed on patterns with grain lines matching and following manufacturer's directions. Cut out the shapes on traced lines.

Remove paper backing from shapes. Referring to photo for placement, place shapes right side up on front of sweatshirt, overlapping shapes as shown on pattern. Fuse shapes in place.

If desired, use quilter's marking pen or pencil to draw light string on front of sweatshirt.

Separate six-strand floss and

thread embroidery needle with three strands of floss or thread needle with a single strand of black pearl cotton. Backstitch light string, mouth on tree, eyebrows and around eyes. Blanket-stitch around all remaining shapes. See Fig. 1 below left for stitch illustrations.

Sew the star button to top of tree.

Referring to pattern for placement, use black fabric marker or black dimensional paint to add a small dot to each eye. Let dry. ✪

APPLIQUE KEY

— Cutting/stitching line
- - - Overlapped portion of pattern
↔ Direction of grain

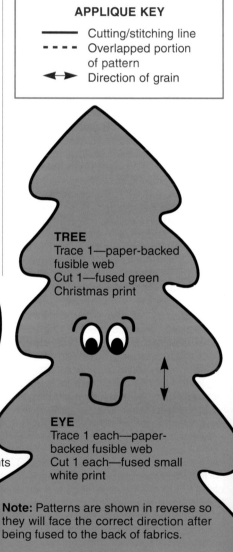

TREE
Trace 1—paper-backed fusible web
Cut 1—fused green Christmas print

EYE
Trace 1 each—paper-backed fusible web
Cut 1 each—fused small white print

LIGHTBULB BASE
Trace 14—paper-backed fusible web
Cut 14—fused small gold print

LIGHTBULB
Trace 14—paper-backed fusible web
Cut 2 each—fused small blue, green, orange, purple, red, white and yellow prints

Note: Patterns are shown in reverse so they will face the correct direction after being fused to the back of fabrics.

Fig. 1
Blanket stitch

Backstitch

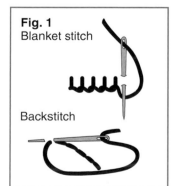

Fashion a Festive New Look With Merry Beads and Bows

wire cutters to cut wire even with beads at end of Rows 3 and 4.

Gently press on wired ends to form the beaded circle into a wreath shape as shown in photo.

Attach a jump ring to center of any row of beading and to loop on earring. Use needle-nose pliers to close jump ring.

Thread red ribbon around front wire edge of wreath opposite jump ring. Tie ribbon in a small bow. Trim ribbon ends as desired.

Repeat to make second earring.

Give the pair to a friend or wear them yourself this Christmas! ✛

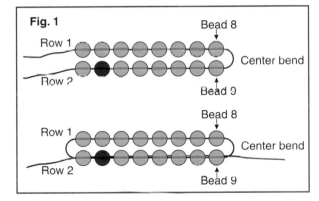

Fig. 1

RING IN the season and round out any holiday outfit in Yuletide style with these sparkly wreath earrings. Janet Shipley Hawks of Tulsa, Oklahoma fashioned them from transparent seed beads to catch all the lights and colors of Christmas, then trimmed each with a tiny red bow.

"They work up in no time and make great stocking stuffers or last-minute gifts to share with teachers and friends," Janet suggests.

Materials Needed:
Chart on this page
Size 10/0 transparent seed beads—300 green and 52 red
Two shallow rimmed containers
34-gauge gold beading wire
One pair of pierced or clip-on earrings with loops
Two 5mm gold jump rings
Two 10-inch lengths of 1/16-inch-wide red satin ribbon
Wire cutters
Needle-nose pliers
Scissors

Finished Size: Each earring measures about 1 inch across.

Directions:
Refer to chart at far right for colors of

beads in each row when adding beads. Keep all beads in each row close together.

Pour green beads into one container and red beads into the other container.

Cut a 36-in. length of beading wire. String 14 green beads, one red bead and one green bead on wire.

Center beads on wire. Bend wire sharply between beads 8 and 9, making two rows of beads with eight beads in each row. Insert Row 1 wire from left to right through all eight beads in Row 2 as shown in Fig. 1 above.

Bend left wire to the right below second row. Working from left to right, add five green beads, one red bead and two green beads as shown on Row 3 of chart. Insert right wire of Row 2 from right to left through all beads in Row 3.

In the same way, continue to follow chart through Row 22, adding beads to the longest wire and inserting the wire of previous row through the row of beads just added.

To end beading, insert right wire from Row 22 from right to left through all beads in Row 1 and left wire from Row 22 from left to right through all beads in Row 2. Draw up wire so Rows 1 and 22 meet to form a circle.

Then insert wire from Row 1 through all beads in Row 3 and insert wire from Row 2 through all beads in Row 4. Use

BEADING CHART

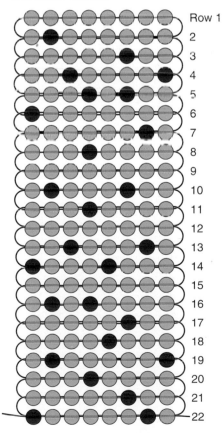

Kids Will Take a Shine To 'Pop' Art Gift Trims

Dimensional craft/fabric paints—black, brown, dark green, red and white
Textured snow medium
Small flat paintbrush
Toothpick
Large hand-sewing needle
1/8-inch round paper punch (optional)
White all-purpose thread or clear monofilament thread
Scissors

Finished Size: Candy cane ornament is 2-1/2 inches wide x 4 inches long. Gingerbread boy is 3-1/8 inches wide x 4 inches long. Stocking is 3-1/8 inches wide x 3-3/4 inches long.

Directions:
Remove label from soda bottle, then cut off and discard bottom of bottle. Wash and dry bottle.

Trace patterns onto individual pieces of tracing paper with marker.

Tape each pattern to the inside of the soda bottle, positioning them so pattern

SODA BOTTLE TRIM PATTERNS
Trace 1 each—tracing paper
Cut 1 each—clear plastic
Paint each as directed
O = hole for hanging loop

lines do not overlap. On the outside of the bottle, trace over outlines of each pattern with marker. If desired, use marker to trace over inside design lines of each pattern. Use rubbing alcohol and a cotton swab to remove any unwanted lines or markings.

Cut out each shape from plastic bottle, cutting just inside traced outlines.

Use paper punch or hand-sewing needle to make a hole in each ornament where shown on patterns for hanger.

PAINTING: Keep paper towels and a container of water handy to clean brush. Place dabs of each acrylic paint color on foam plate or palette as needed. Acrylic paints are applied to the back (inside) of each shape. Let paint dry after every application.

Keep the tip of the bottle above the surface when applying dimensional paint. Dimensional paints are applied to the front (outside) of each shape. Use toothpick to break any bubbles in dimensional paint and to smooth out un-

YOUNGSTERS will take pride in making *and* giving these jolly tie-on gift or tree trims. "They're so quick and easy to do," writes crafter Carol Brandon of Uxbridge, Ontario. "I've even made them with first graders."

And Santa himself would never guess such bright and sparkly trims are fashioned from only plastic soda bottles and a little Christmas magic!

Materials Needed (for all):
Patterns on this page and next page
Tracing paper
Black permanent marker
One liter-size clear plastic soda bottle
Rubbing alcohol
Cotton swabs (optional)
Tape
Paper towels
Water container
Waxed paper
Foam plate or palette
Acrylic craft paints—brown, dark green, red, silver metallic and white

CANDY CANE

STOCKING

even areas. Remove any unwanted paint while it is still wet with a damp paintbrush or cotton swab.

Place ornaments on waxed paper while painting and drying.

Refer to photo and patterns as a guide while painting as directed in the instructions that follow.

Candy cane: Use flat brush and red and white acrylic paint to paint stripes on the back of the candy cane. Add additional coats of paint until the paint is opaque.

Use flat brush and silver metallic acrylic paint to paint entire back.

Use red dimensional paint to outline each red section on the front of the candy cane. Let dry.

Use white dimensional paint to outline outer edges on the front of each white area. Let dry.

Gingerbread boy: Use flat brush and brown acrylic paint to paint entire back of gingerbread. Add additional coats of paint until the paint is opaque.

Use flat brush and silver metallic acrylic paint to paint entire back.

Use brown dimensional paint to outline the front. Let dry.

Use white dimensional paint to add wavy frosting lines to the front. Let dry.

Use black dimensional paint to add eyes, nose, mouth and buttons to the front. Let dry.

Stocking: Use flat brush and white acrylic paint to paint cuff on back of stocking.

Use the flat brush and dark green acrylic paint to paint heel and toe on back.

Use flat brush and red acrylic paint to paint remaining areas on back.

Use flat brush and silver metallic acrylic paint to paint entire back.

Use dark green dimensional paint to outline the toe and heel shapes on the front. Let dry.

Use red dimensional paint to outline the red areas on the front. Let dry.

Use flat brush to apply a thick layer of textured snow to front of cuff. Let dry.

FINISHING: Thread hand-sewing needle with a 10-in. length of thread. Insert needle through holes at tops of ornaments. Remove needle and tie thread ends together to form a loop for hanging on Christmas tree.

GINGERBREAD BOY

Starry Holders Twinkle Brightly

LOOKING FOR a quick-and-easy gift idea? Crafter Helen Rafson came up with one that brightens her own Louisville, Kentucky home—glass votive holders frosted with stars.

"Stencils and gloss paint make these so easy," Helen explains. "I scatter the holders around my house and keep several on hand as last-minute gifts for drop-in guests."

Materials Needed (for all):
Three 2-5/8-inch-tall clear glass votive holders
Vinegar
Cotton balls
Several 1/2-inch-high gummed foil stars
1/4-inch-wide masking tape
Small piece of household sponge
Foam plate or palette
White acrylic gloss craft paint (Helen used DecoArt Ultra Gloss paint)
Three votive or tea light candles
Scissors

Finished Size: Each votive holder measures 2 inches across x 2-5/8 inches high.

Directions:
Use a cotton ball and vinegar to clean the outside of each votive holder. Let dry.

Referring to photo for position, randomly adhere stars to one votive holder.

Cut and apply four strips of masking tape vertically to outside of another votive holder, spacing them equally around the holder. Adhere three stars to each open section.

Cut and apply a strip of masking tape around the top and bottom edges of the third votive holder and adhere stars as desired.

Pour a small puddle of white paint onto foam plate or palette. Dampen sponge and dip into paint, then blot sponge on a clean area of plate or palette to remove excess paint. Using an up-and-down motion, sponge-paint around sides of each votive holder. Let dry.

Carefully remove stars and strips of masking tape.

Place votive or tea light candle inside each holder—and light up your holiday nights!

Plug into Warmth of Holly Days With Thrifty, Nifty Snow Buddy

LIGHT UP your holidays with this merry snow buddy crafted from a recycled lightbulb and swaddled in whatever cuddly fleece scraps you have on hand.

Designer Bette Veinot from Bridgewater, Nova Scotia includes easy-to-follow directions and suggests making several. "Why not glue them to wreaths and swags? Or you could add a hanger to each and tuck them among the branches of your tree," she says.

Materials Needed:
Pattern on next page
Pencil
Standard lightbulb
Foam plate or palette
Paper towels
Water container
Acrylic craft paints—black, dark orange, dusty rose and white
Paintbrushes—small round, small flat, liner and 1-inch foam brush
Burgundy Polarfleece or other high-loft fleece—4-3/4-inch x 8-inch piece for hat, 1-1/2-inch x 12-inch strip for bow and 1-inch x 2-1/2-inch strip for center of bow
Burgundy all-purpose thread
Hand-sewing needle
Small amount of polyester stuffing
1/2-inch gold metallic button
18-inch length of 1/8-inch-wide burgundy-and-gold metallic ribbon for bow on hat
Two 2-inch squares of dark green pin-dot fabric
1-1/2-inch square of paper-backed fusible web
6-inch length of 1/8-inch burgundy-and-gold metallic cord for trim on hat
1/4-inch berries for trim—two gold and one burgundy
6-inch length of heavy gold metallic thread for hanger
Ruler
Iron and ironing surface
Low-temperature glue gun and glue sticks
Scissors

Finished Size: Ornament is about 3-1/2 inches across x 7 inches high without hanger.

Directions:
Trace holly pattern on next page twice onto paper side of fusible web, leaving 1/2 in. between shapes.

Center and fuse shapes onto wrong side of one 2-in. square of dark green pin-dot fabric following manufacturer's directions. Cut out when cool, cutting just outside traced lines of each.

Remove paper backing. Fuse holly leaves onto wrong side of remaining 2-in. square of fabric. Cut out holly leaves, cutting just inside previously cut edge of each.

PAINTING: Keep paper towel and a container of water handy to clean brushes. Place dabs of each paint color onto foam plate or palette as needed.

Add coats of paint as needed for complete coverage. Let paint dry after every application.

Refer to photo and painting diagram on next page as a guide while painting as directed in the instructions that follow.

Use foam brush and white to paint lightbulb.

Measure 2-1/4 in. from metal base of lightbulb. Use pencil to draw nose, eyes and mouth on lightbulb freehand.

Use round brush and dark orange to paint nose.

Dip flat brush into dusty rose and wipe on paper towel to remove excess paint. With a circular motion, add cheeks.

Use liner and black to paint two small eyes. Add two tiny black lashes at outer corner of each eye. With same brush and black, add a very thin eyebrow above each eye.

Use liner and black to add mouth. Then outline nose with black and add inside design lines.

Use liner and white to add highlights to eyes.

HAT: Fold 3/4 in. along one long edge of 4-3/4-in. x 8-in. piece of burgundy fleece to right side for band of hat. Glue lightly along center of band to hold.

With band on outside, wrap hat around lightbulb and overlap short ends in the back. Without gluing hat to lightbulb, glue overlapped portion as needed to hold.

Position hat on lightbulb with lower edge of band above face as shown in photo, bringing sides and back down around lightbulb and making sure top of hat extends about 1/2 in. above end of metal base. Carefully glue lower edge of band to lightbulb as needed to hold.

Thread hand-sewing needle with a double strand of burgundy thread. Sew around top of hat about 3/4 in. from raw edge with a running stitch. See Fig. 1 on next page for stitch illustration.

Stuff hat lightly with stuffing up to base of lightbulb. Pull thread to gather fleece around base of lightbulb. Fasten off thread.

Wrap burgundy-and-gold metallic ribbon around top of hat and tie in a bow in front. Trim ends of ribbon as desired and tie each end in an overhand knot.

Handy Tip

TO GIVE your Snow Buddy an even more authentic look, try adding a layer of textured snow to the lightbulb after applying white paint. Then lightly draw on facial features and paint as directed above.

Glue holly leaves and gold and burgundy berries to center of bow.

Glue length of burgundy-and-gold metallic cord centered around hat above top of band. Tuck and glue ends under fold of band.

Fold the 1-1/2-in. x 12-in. burgundy fleece strip as shown in Fig. 2 below for bow. Wrap center of bow with the 1-in. x 2-1/2-in. piece of fleece and overlap ends on back of bow. Glue as needed to hold. Glue bow to bottom of lightbulb. Trim ends as desired.

Glue gold metallic button to center of bow.

Glue ends of heavy gold metallic thread to opposite sides of lightbulb base for hanger.

Display on your tree or wreath during the holidays!

HOLLY PATTERN
Trace 2—paper-backed fusible web
Cut 2 as directed—fused dark green
   pin-dot fabric

PAINTING DIAGRAM

Fig. 1 Running stitch

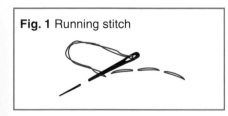

Fig. 2 Making fleece bow

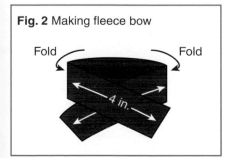

Fold   Fold

4 in.

Dressed-Up Jar Is Endeering

RUDOLPH packs plenty of holiday cheer with this whimsical gift jar from Lenora Schut of Pella, Iowa.

"My boys make these from empty nondairy creamer containers and fill them with hot cocoa mix for relatives at Christmas," Lenora says. You could also pack one with peppermints and tuck them in a basket with mugs and microwave popcorn.

Materials Needed:
Pattern on this page
Tracing paper and pencil
Empty 16-ounce brown plastic
   container (Lenora used a nondairy
   creamer container)
6-inch x 10-inch piece of brown craft
   foam
Two 18mm glue-on wiggle eyes
One 1-inch red pom-pom
2-Inch x 20-inch strip of red-and-green
   plaid fabric
Small artificial poinsettia
Low-temperature glue gun and glue
   sticks
Scissors

Finished Size: Reindeer gift jar measures about 8-3/4 inches across x 11 inches tall.

Directions:
Trace antler pattern onto tracing paper. Cut out pattern on traced lines.

Trace around pattern twice onto craft foam with pencil. Cut out antlers, cutting just inside traced lines.

Remove the label and any label residue from plastic container. Clean and dry container.

Referring to photo for placement, glue eyes to one side of container about 2-1/2 in. from top. Glue pom-pom centered about 1/2 in. below eyes.

Tie fabric strip into a bow. Glue bow to container below nose. Trim ends of bow as desired.

Glue poinsettia to top of lid.

Glue antlers to back of container about 1 in. down from the top, positioning them as shown in photo.

Fill container with goodies or cocoa mix—then try to keep the lid on this great gift idea!

ANTLER PATTERN
Trace 1—tracing paper
Cut 2, reversing 1—brown craft foam

'Yule' Take Boughs with This Elegant, Easy Table Topper!

SPRUCE UP your mantel or serve up the season's best for holiday dinner guests with this simple but elegantly festive centerpiece.

Jean Devore wove together scented candles, evergreens, colorful fruits, berries and pinecones to create this Christmas masterpiece for her Jackson, Missouri home. Use her easy instructions and your on-hand craft supplies to salute the season in holiday style.

Materials Needed:
Metal candle holder with three pillar candle stands*
48-inch length of artificial wired pine garland
2 yards of 1-inch-wide metallic gold striped ribbon
Artificial fruit-and-pinecone picks and berry picks

Three pillar candles in color of choice
Craft wire
Wire cutters
Scissors

*Jean used an 18-inch-long tiered metal candle holder. You can use any candle holder you like to create a similar look. If you can't find a tiered version that holds three pillar candles, you can use three separate candle holders instead.

Finished Size: Including candles, table decor measures about 12 inches high x 30 inches long.

Directions:
Fold length of wired pine garland in half. Intertwine garland around candle holder, wrapping ends of individual boughs around candle holder as needed to hold.

Use wire cutters to cut stems of artificial fruit-and-pinecone picks and berry picks to desired length. Use ends of stems or craft wire to secure trims to garland where desired.

Referring to Fig. 1, form ribbon into a multi-loop bow that measures about 6 inches across. Attach bow to the garland with a length of craft wire. Trim the ends of bow as desired.

Add candles and top your table with this fine pine decoration! ✤

Fig. 1 Making multi-loop bow

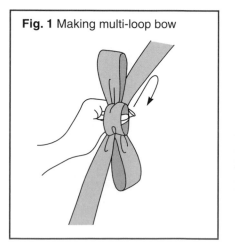

Merry Mounts Trim Tree in High-Stepping Holiday Style!

YOU'LL REIN in a sleighful of compliments with these prancing, dancing little horses! They're as bright as can be in their shiny ribbons and flowery trims.

Crafted from felt by Linda Bloomgren of Minneapolis, Minnesota, they add a festive touch of Scandinavian color and "country" to any holiday tree, she says. Follow Linda's easy directions to stitch up a spirited herd of your own!

Materials Needed (for one):
Patterns on this page
Tracing paper and pencil
Felt—two 6-inch squares of blue, gold or red for body of horse and scraps each of green, red and white for leaves, flowers and flower centers
All-purpose thread to match body of horse
Hand-sewing needle
Polyester stuffing
3-inch length of 1/8-inch-wide green or red satin ribbon
5mm glue-on wiggle eye
8-inch length of gold metallic thread for hanger
White (tacky) glue
Ruler or measuring tape
Scissors

Finished Size: Each horse is about 5-1/4 inches long x 5-1/2 inches high.

Directions:
Trace patterns on this page onto tracing paper with pencil.

Place both 6-in. squares of felt together with wrong sides facing and edges matching. Pin body pattern to layered felt. Cut out body, cutting through both layers of felt on traced lines of pattern. Remove pattern.

Thread hand-sewing needle with a single strand of thread to match body of horse. Sew around outer edges of body with a long deep whipstitch, inserting stuffing between the layers as you sew. See Fig. 1 (below left) for stitch illustration.

Cut out ear from matching felt.

Cut out flowers, flower centers and leaves from felt as directed on the patterns.

Referring to photo for position, glue ear to top of head. Glue flowers and leaves to same side of horse's body. Glue a flower center to each flower.

Cut a 1-3/4-in. length of satin ribbon. Referring to photo for placement, glue ribbon down one side of head of horse. Center and glue remaining length of ribbon across bottom of first ribbon. Trim excess ribbon even with the sides of the head.

Glue eye to same side of head where shown on pattern.

Thread hand-sewing needle with length of gold metallic thread. Insert needle through top of body about 5/8 in. from back of head. Remove needle and tie thread ends to form hanging loop. ✦

HORSE TRIM PATTERNS

EAR
Trace 1—tracing paper
Cut 1—color of felt to match body of horse

HORSE
Trace 1—tracing paper
Cut as directed—blue, gold or red felt

FLOWER
Trace 1—tracing paper
Cut 3—white felt

FLOWER CENTER
Trace 1—tracing paper
Cut 3—gold or red felt

LEAF
Trace 1—tracing paper
Cut 6—green felt

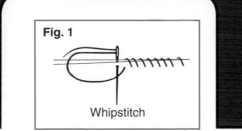

Fig. 1

Whipstitch

Crochet Some Floral Flair For Holiday Table Settings

PLANT these pretty poinsettia place mats and napkin rings around your table and watch the Yuletide feelings blossom among your guests!

Emma Willey of Winston, Oregon crocheted the nostalgic table trimmers in traditional Christmas colors. "The combination of stitches is fun to do," she says. "Anyone who has crocheted before will enjoy this design."

Materials Needed:
3-ply bulky-weight yarn—6 ounces of green and 3 ounces of white (Emma used Aunt Lydia's Craft and Rug yarn)
4-ply worsted-weight yarn—1 ounce of red
Crochet hooks—size I/9 (5.5mm) for place mat and napkin ring and size E/4 (3.5mm) for poinsettias
Yarn or tapestry needle
Scissors

Gauge: Using Size I crochet hook, 3 scs and 3 rows = 1 inch. Slight variations in gauge will change the finished size a bit.

Finished Size: Each place mat measures about 12 inches wide x 18 inches long. Each napkin ring measures about 2 inches wide x 1-1/2 inches high.

Directions:
PLACE MAT (make two): Row 1: With green yarn and size I crochet hk, ch 50, sc in eighth ch from hk (counts as end

hdc and ch-sp), ch 2, sk next 2 chs, sc in next ch, * ch 4, sk next 2 chs, sc in next ch, ch 2, sk next 2 chs, sc in next ch; repeat from * to last 3 chs, ch 2, sk next 2 chs, hdc in last ch: 15 ch-sps.

Row 2: Ch 1, turn, sc in ch-2 sp, * work 4 dcs in next ch-2 sp, sc in next ch-4 sp; repeat from * across, ch 4, turn: 28 dcs and 8 scs.

Row 3: Sc in first dc, ch 2, sk next 2 dcs, sc in next dc, * ch 4, sk next sc, sc in next dc, ch 2, sk next 2 dcs, sc in next dc; repeat from * across to last sc, ch 2, hdc in last sc: 7 ch-4 sps and 8 ch-2 sps.

Repeat Rows 2 and 3 until work measures about 17-1/2 in., ending with a Row 2. Do not fasten off.

Edging: Round 1: Ch 1, turn, sc around, working 1 sc in each st across narrow end, 3 scs in each corner, 1 sc in ends of each row and 2 scs in hdc and ch-sps around; join with a sl st in first sc of round. Fasten off.

Round 2: With a white slip knot on hk, sc in any sc, ch 2, sk 1 sc, * sc in next sc, ch 2, sk 1 sc; repeat from * around, join with a sl st in first sc. Fasten off.

Large Poinsettia (make two): With red yarn and size E crochet hk, ch 6, join with a sl st in first ch made to form a ring, * ch 6, sc in second ch from hk, hdc in each of the next 2 chs, dc in each of the next 2 chs, sc in ring; repeat from * five more times. Fasten off, leaving a tail of yarn.

Small Poinsettia (make four): With red yarn and size E crochet hk, ch 6, join

with a sl st in first ch made, forming a ring, * ch 4, sc in second ch from hk, hdc in next ch, dc in next ch, sc in ring; repeat from * five more times. Fasten off, leaving a tail of yarn.

Finishing: Use yarn or tapestry needle and yarn ends to tack one large and two small poinsettias to lower right corner of each place mat.

Thread yarn or tapestry needle with white yarn. Add three French knots to the center of each poinsettia. See Fig. 1 for stitch illustration.

Use yarn or tapestry needle to weave in all loose ends.

NAPKIN RING (make two): Row 1: With green yarn and size I crochet hk, ch 7, dc in fourth ch from hk and in each remaining ch, ch 3, turn: count 4 dcs.

Row 2: Dc in each dc across, ch 3, turn: 4 dcs.

Rows 3-9: Repeat Row 2: 4 dcs. Fasten off at end of Row 9, leaving a tail of yarn.

Thread tail of yarn onto yarn or tapestry needle. With edges matching, sew narrow ends together to form a ring.

Poinsettia: (make two): With red yarn and size E crochet hk, ch 6, join with a sl st in first ch made to form a ring, * ch 4, sc in second ch from hk, hdc in next ch, dc in next ch, sc in ring; repeat from * five more times. Fasten off, leaving a tail of yarn.

Finishing: Use yarn or tapestry needle and yarn ends to tack one small poinsettia to each napkin ring, covering seam.

Thread yarn or tapestry needle with white yarn. Stitch three French knots to the center of each poinsettia. Use yarn or tapestry needle to weave in all loose ends.

Deck your place settings with style!

Fig. 1

French knot

ABBREVIATIONS

ch(s)	chain(s)
dc(s)	double crochet(s)
hdc(s)	half double crochet(s)
hk	hook
sc(s)	single crochet(s)
sl st	slip stitch
sk	skip
sp(s)	space(s)
st(s)	stitch(es)
*	Instructions following asterisk are repeated as directed.

I'll Never Forget...

Memories of Christmases Past Still Linger and Shine

By B.D. Clemens of Somonauk, Illinois

WHENEVER the glitz and clatter of the holiday season start to clutter my mind, I remember my childhood days—and everything comes back into focus.

From the age of 8, I lived with my grandparents on a rocky hill farm in Webster County, Missouri. Grandpa made his living growing an annual crop of tomatoes and hand-milking five or six mixed-breed cows.

We had no electricity and drew our water from the well. The house was heated with woodstoves, one in the living room and another in the kitchen.

Grandpa farmed with mules and horses—and for playmates, I had dogs, cats, chickens and turkeys.

Our farm was dotted with cedar trees of all sizes. During the year, I'd diligently search for the perfect Christmas tree whenever I played in the fields. Once I found the right one, I'd visit it again and again so I could be sure to find it when winter was upon us.

Then, come December, I'd lead Grandpa right to it. But no matter if I chose a big, little, fat or tall tree, through Grandpa's gentle persuasion, we somehow seemed to end up with just about the same size cedar every year.

Since so many were close to the house, we seldom had to hitch up the wagon. Grandpa dragged it home with the rope while I carried the ax and saw.

Before we took it into the house, we stopped at the woodpile so Grandpa could nail on a stand. Then we shook it out good. Grandma didn't want any needles or old bird nests falling on her floor.

Sweet Memories

She always approved our choice and had the boxes of decorations open and ready. There were garlands of silver tinsel, glass balls in all colors, cloth candy canes, snowflakes, and a shiny tin star for the very top.

As we decorated the tree, Grandpa popped corn on top of the big heating stove. Then Grandma made a pan of candy using only sugar and water. When it cooled, it was milky white and so sweet it hurt your teeth. We'd break off slim pieces to suck as we strung the popcorn with needle and thread.

If there was enough popcorn left over, Grandma made popcorn balls with molasses. Grandpa was very partial to popcorn balls.

Job Well Done

We finished trimming the evergreen by winding the strings of popcorn around the tree and draping each branch with slivers of tinsel. After Grandpa placed the tin star on top, we stood back to admire our work.

Grandma always hugged me and said how beautiful it was, and Grandpa always complimented me on my choice of tree. I recall feeling very proud.

I remember there were some fantastic toys—even a fancy Radio Flyer wagon one time—tucked under those trees over the years, along with all kinds of socks, mittens, belts and sweaters.

During the second week of January, we'd take the tree down. Decorations were stored back in their boxes, the popcorn was fed to the chickens, and Grandpa threw the tree into a ditch near the house, on top of other trees from Christmases past.

That ditch emptied into the pasture, and sometimes, during the hot days of summer while bringing in the cows for milking, I'd find little strips of tinsel in the grass...and remember Christmas.

Caroling Party's in Tune with Season

WHAT BETTER way to voice your holiday spirit and celebrate Christmas than with an old-time caroling party?

Whether you gather with friends, family members, a Scout troop, church group or neighbors, all ages can take part in "trolling the ancient Yuletide carols" that help make Christmas merry.

Best of all, it doesn't take a lot of fancy food, frills or fussing to put on a party that's fa-la-la festive for all!

A hot beverage and steaming crockpot entree are sure to take the chill off your frosty songsters. And you'll warm to the idea that both can be prepared ahead of time at your convenience, then set on simmer until guests are hungry.

We've included two simple but sure-fire recipes here, for a tangy Caroling Cider and tasty Sloppy Joes.

Instead, you might opt for a progressive caroling party to share hosting chores and keep folks moving from house to house. One hostess might serve the appetizers, another the entree, still another eggnog, cookies and desserts.

We've included a sheet of familiar carol lyrics (opposite) for you. So dash off some quick copies, distribute to your guests and have yourself a merry little caroling party!

CAROLING CIDER

> 2 quarts apple cider *or* juice
> 2 cups cranberry juice
> 3 tablespoons brown sugar
> 1-1/2 teaspoons lemon juice
> 1/8 teaspoon ground nutmeg
> 1 cinnamon stick (3 inches)

In a 5-qt. slow cooker, combine the cider, cranberry juice, brown sugar, lemon juice and nutmeg. Add the cinnamon stick. Cover and cook on low for 2-4 hours. Discard cinnamon stick and stir cider before serving. **Yield:** 2-1/2 quarts.

SLOPPY JOES

> 2 pounds ground beef
> 1 large onion, chopped
> 1 garlic clove, minced
> 1-1/2 cups ketchup
> 1 can (8 ounces) tomato sauce
> 2/3 cup packed brown sugar
> 1/2 cup sweet pickle relish
> 1 tablespoon prepared
>   mustard
> 1 teaspoon Worcestershire
>   sauce
> 16 hamburger buns, split

In a Dutch oven, cook the beef, onion and garlic over medium heat until meat is no longer pink; drain. Stir in the ketchup, tomato sauce, brown sugar, pickle relish, mustard and Worcestershire sauce; mix well.

Simmer, uncovered, for 20 minutes or until heated through. Keep warm in a slow cooker if desired. Spoon on-to buns. **Yield:** 16 servings.

WE WISH YOU A MERRY CHRISTMAS

We wish you a Merry Christmas;
We wish you a Merry Christmas;
We wish you a Merry Christmas
And a Happy New Year.

CHORUS:
Good tidings to you,
Wherever you are;
Good tidings for Christmas and a
Happy New Year.

Oh, bring us a figgy pudding;
Oh, bring us a figgy pudding;
Oh, bring us a figgy pudding
And a cup of good cheer.

REPEAT CHORUS

JOY TO THE WORLD

Joy to the world!
The Lord is come,
Let earth receive her King!
Let every heart prepare Him room,
And heav'n and nature sing,
And heav'n and nature sing,
And heav'n and heav'n and
nature sing.

Joy to the earth!
The Savior reigns,
Let men their songs employ,
While fields and floods,
Rocks, hills and plains,
Repeat the sounding joy,
Repeat the sounding joy,
Repeat, repeat the sounding joy.

SILENT NIGHT

Silent night, holy night,
All is calm, all is bright.
'Round yon Virgin Mother
and Child,
Holy infant so tender and mild,
Sleep in heavenly peace.
Sleep in heavenly peace.

Silent night, holy night,
Shepherds quake at the sight.
Glories stream from heaven afar,
Heav'nly hosts sing Alleluia;
Christ the Savior is born.
Christ the Savior is born.

DECK THE HALLS

Deck the halls with boughs
of holly,
Fa la la la la, la la la la.
'Tis the season to be jolly,
Fa la la la la, la la la la.

Don we now our gay apparel,
Fa la la, la la la, la la la.
Troll the ancient Yuletide carol,
Fa la la la la, la la la la.

See the blazing Yule before us,
Fa la la la la, la la la la.
Strike the harp and join the chorus.
Fa la la la la, la la la la.

Follow me in merry measure,
Fa la la, la la la, la la la.
While I tell of Yuletide treasure,
Fa la la la la, la la la la.

JOLLY OLD ST. NICHOLAS

Jolly Old St. Nicholas,
Lean your ear this way!
Don't you tell a single soul,
What I'm going to say;
Christmas Eve is coming soon;
Now, you dear old man,
Whisper what you'll bring to me:
Tell me if you can.

When the clock is striking twelve,
When I'm fast asleep,
Down the chimney broad and black
With your pack you'll creep;
All the stockings you will find
Hanging in a row;
Mine will be the shortest one,
You'll be sure to know.

AWAY IN A MANGER

Away in a manger,
No crib for His bed,
The little Lord Jesus
Lay down His sweet head.
The stars in the sky
Looked down where He lay
The little Lord Jesus,
Asleep on the hay.

Be near me, Lord Jesus,
I ask Thee to stay,
Close by me forever,
And love me, I pray!
Bless all the dear children
In Thy tender care,
And take us to heaven,
To live with Thee there.

Once Upon a Grapevine Wreath...

We've gathered a trio of low-cost twists on a high-spirited holiday standby!

HAS THE CHRISTMAS countdown left you short on time and money but long on last-minute to-do lists and decorating dreams?

What a comfort to know it doesn't take hours, fresh greens (or even a lot of green!) to fashion fast festive wreaths that welcome visitors to your home in holiday style.

Snippets of ribbon, scraps of fabric and a dash of imagination can turn inexpensive grapevine wreaths into simple but striking symbols of Christmas spirit for any room in your house.

As an example, we decked these 14-inch wreaths three different ways for three different rooms, using little more than a glue gun and some at-hand seasonal odds and ends.

For the Kitchen

Red gingham ribbon twirled and tied in a big bow cooks up a hearth-warming country look for the wreath above!

Silver tea balls and measuring spoons add holiday sparkle and shine. Cinnamon sticks tied with red raffia lend a spicy scent tucked among jolly Christmas cookie cutters.

For a fun finishing touch, try penning some whimsical recipe cards for "Reindeer Treats", "Elf Snacks" and "Santa Sugarplums".

Powder Room Pretty

Christmas is a time for memories and surprises in unlikely places. Brighten your guest bath with a seaside theme that combines beachcombing memories with special treasures collected on family vacations.

We freshened up our wreath (pic-tured below left) with starfish and tiny tulle bags filled with sweet-smelling potpourri, then gave it all a wash of gala gold and red ribbon. You could also use seashells, sand dollars or small pieces of driftwood and beach glass.

Merry Musical Accent

Invite carolers and neighbors to warm up in a front hall echoing with the joyful sounds of the season.

Shiny brass jingle bells, horns and little toy drums blend with tiny scrolls of sheet music, sprigs of holly and a fes-tive holiday bow to trim the wreath above and trumpet "Happy Holidays"!

Wreath Roundup

HERE are a few more fun ways to decorate a holiday wreath...

- Artificial evergreen garlands woven through or wrapped around the vines are an easy way to add color and depth.
- Wrap with ribbon or lights before attaching any trims.
- Begin with larger trims first, then fill in the spaces with smaller ones.
- Add all of one material at a time, spacing it out evenly around the wreath for an arrangement that's balanced and bright.

Nativity Scenes Bring Home True Meaning of Holy Night

COME CHRISTMAS, there's sure to be plenty of "room at the inn" in the Ashland, Ohio home of Nancy Watson —even though all six rooms are filled to the brim with her cherished collection of Nativity scenes!

"There's even a Nativity sun catcher on my shower door in the bath," she says with a laugh.

Nancy started collecting her Christmas treasures about 37 years ago.

"Why? Well, the way I see it, there are two reasons for this special season. Christ's birthday is what Christmas really is about —despite all the commercialism. And I love to decorate with that in mind," she says.

Her first Nativity was made of glass with a little mirror underneath, she recalls. "But my favorite one today is probably the white porcelain set a friend at church made," she notes. "I like it because it's the most versatile. I can set it out on red or green or any color, really, and it looks nice."

That's important when you're try-ing to find a place for 50-some Nativity scenes!

"The packing and unpacking every year is the only downside," Nancy admits. "That and the fact that I'm running out of space to store them all! I bring them out at Thanksgiving and have to take down all my other knickknacks to make room."

Nancy was forced to downsize her collection when she moved to a smaller home several years ago. "But what's left are my very favorites," she explains.

That includes the large clay Nativity hanging on one wall, a manger scene cross-stitched by her daughter-in-law on another, a table full of musical Nativity snow globes and a colorful Mexican version from a long-ago pen pal.

There's also a set small enough to fit in one hand, Nativity afghans and pillows on the couch and a paper-and-copper trifold Nativity screen catching the light in one window. Doilies recalling the first Noel dress her bedroom…Nativity pins fill her jewelry box!

Still more Nativity scenes made from pewter, glass, wood and porcelain fill tables, perch on windowsills and top bureaus and bookshelves. Even the kitchen table is graced with a large Nativity cookie jar.

Outside her front door, a Nativity flag proclaims "Joy to the World". Inside, Nancy's tree is filled with Christmas ornaments depicting the night of Jesus' birth—many of them made by her own two boys when they were growing up.

"There are so many good memories tied up with each one of my Nativity scenes," Nancy reflects. "Each holds wonderful sweet memories of family and friends. Oh, yes—and that's the second reason for this beautiful season!"

Her 'Pet' Project Makes for Some Tasty Holiday Treats

CHRISTMAS IS going to the dogs at Inge Schermerhorn's house. And she couldn't be more pleased!

This country mother of four grown children is the owner of Bone-A-Fido Treats, a small gourmet dog biscuit company she operates from her home in East Kingston, New Hampshire.

Inge, a blue-ribbon cook in her own right, whipped up her first batch of bone-shaped dog biscuits for the family collie, "McDivot", years ago.

"My two sons were babies at the time and needed a lot of attention," she recalls. "I was looking for something fun to do with my two older girls so they wouldn't feel left out."

The doggie treats were such a success with the family pooch that Inge was inspired to bake up 200 more for sale at a store she owned with her husband, John.

"Everyone thought it was a joke and said they'd never sell," Inge recalls. "But those biscuits were totally gone by the end of the day."

She continued making the crunchy treats for McDivot and noticed, along with his veterinarian, a marked improvement in the dog's teeth and gums. But for the next few years, Inge's "pet project" got buried in the bustle of full-time mothering.

Then in 1996, she decided to take another look at her gourmet dog biscuit recipe, tweak it a bit and market it as a bake-your-own mix. Sales since then prove she's hit upon a popular idea!

Packaged in a brown bag tied up with a twist of twine and a cute bone-shaped cookie cutter, her Bone-A-Fido Treats mix is now available at several New England pet and specialty stores

and also through the mail. "It's really been taking off," Inge says with pride.

Only wholesome all-natural ingredients go into her gourmet mix, including unbleached and whole wheat flours, cracked wheat, cornmeal, chicken-flavored granules and peanuts (to fight "doggie breath"). There are no preservatives or extra sugars.

The biscuits couldn't be easier to make, either—just add water, roll the dough, cut out and bake. "And my kids loved helping to make them as much as the dog loved eating them," Inge says.

Editor's Note: *For more information or to order the mix, visit Inge's Web site at www.boneafidotreats.com or call her at 1-866/874-5576, extension 8040.*

BROWN PAPER packages tied up with string ...and topped with a bone-shaped cutter wrap Inge Schermerhorn's dog biscuit mix.

Pet Tips to Try

SOMETIMES, pets can get left behind in the hustle and bustle of the holiday season. Here are a few helpful reminders to make Christmastime safe and fun for your four-footed friend:

• Remind guests not to feed your dog or cat rich food from the dinner table. Greasy scraps can cause stomach upsets.

• Keep your pets away from chocolate candy, alcoholic beverages, gumdrops and popcorn.

• Place holiday plants such as poinsettias and mistletoe out of pets' reach.

• Remember to display candles on high shelves to avoid singed whiskers and burns.

• Secure large Christmas trees to the wall to prevent tipping.

• When working on holiday crafts, keep paints and glues away from pets.

• Wrap up some lessons in kindness to animals along with children's other gifts. Encourage them to include their furry, feathered and four-footed friends in the season's festivities.

• Help youngsters tie a bright yarn loop on a pinecone, spread peanut butter all over it, then roll in birdseed and hang outside a window to feed hungry birds.

• Tie a jingle bell on your cat's collar or a candy cane bandanna or ribbon around your dog's neck!

Oh, Christmas Tree

By Grace Weber of Ellensburg, Washington

"MOM! Everybody's got their tree up. We aren't going to wait until Dad comes home for our tree, are we?"

Danny's eyes are big and eager and catch me off guard. I'd planned on talking about this tree business soon…

"I figured we wouldn't have a tree this year," I begin.

My 10-year-old stops cold.

"No Christmas tree? Why? Everybody has one."

"Well, we're saving up for the new car and need every cent. Plus, Dad won't be back from Grandma and Grandpa's until Christmas Day, and we have too much to do," I explain.

My husband had to go take care of his parents' dairy herd after Grandpa hurt his back, and the timing couldn't have been worse. Between the kids' hectic schedules and my part-time job, not to mention our own farm chores, there was barely an extra second to spare for anything.

Dim Prospects

"We just don't have the time or the money—why, we don't even have lights for the tree! The ones we used last year burned out, so I thought we could skip it this year," I add.

"Oh, but Mom! We've got to…"

Harry, 13, pushes through the kitchen door, dropping his books on the table. "What's going on?"

"Mom won't let us have a Christmas tree!" Danny wails.

"That's crazy. Sure she will," says Harry, heading for the middle cupboard to grab crackers and peanut butter.

I drop into a chair. "Look, we've already spent enough on Christmas, and I can't take any time off," I sigh. "You guys can be grown-up about this. I bet Clara will be."

Clara, our 8-year-old, isn't home yet. We live just outside town and her school bus has a different route than the boys'.

"No, she won't," Harry disagrees. "Little girls love Christmas the most! She's got to have a tree."

"That's enough," I say. This isn't the way I'd hoped things would go.

"Hey, I know," Danny chimes in, "we can cut down that tree out front. It's

got to be just about big enough."

He means my Colorado spruce. It was in sorry shape when I picked it up at a nursery sale, but I cared for it tenderly and it thrived. I love that tree. "No, not my blue spruce!" I sputter.

"*That* would make the prettiest Christmas tree in the county," finishes Harry, triumphant.

Just then Clara comes tramping in, scrubby old winter coat dragging from one arm, a jumble of books in the other.

"What's the matter? Why do you all look so funny?" she asks.

"We're talking about our Christmas tree," Danny announces. "Harry and I are going to cut down that spruce out front so we can decorate it."

Clara's face falls. "No, no. You can't. The little birds…and that nest. We'll never see them again," she wails, recalling the robin's nest, tiny blue eggs and babies from last spring. Tears are dripping down her cheeks. "Not that tree."

"We don't have to decide today," I interrupt. "Let me think about it while you go do your chores."

Harry and Danny shrug their coats on and stomp off to feed our six head of cattle and check on the pigs and riding horses in the corral before cleaning out the stalls. Clara stays behind to help me get supper together.

Dinner is quiet and uneasy. I can't eat. Clara is pouting. We all have something to say but don't dare say it.

Gift of Light

Well before dawn the next day, I sit in the old rocking chair in my bedroom, unable to sleep. The white church steeple gleams in the waning moonlight …and I begin to think that maybe there is a way to turn the blue spruce into a Christmas tree *without* cutting it down.

After I get the kids off to school, I make a phone call. "Reverend Thomas, would the church have any outside Christmas lights not being used this year? I need to borrow some."

"You'll have to come and look," he says. "There's a box full of that stuff in the choir room. Take anything you like."

I head off to work a bit early, stopping at church to look for the lights. I find a box filled with several strands and take it with me.

The hours fly by and soon I'm back home, plugging a heavy outdoor extension cord into our front porch outlet in order to test the lights. Most of the bulbs come to glittering life and I use them to trim the spruce.

Once the tree is lit up, it's beautiful! The needles shine and swish in the light breeze.

Then I peek into the empty robin's nest and remember that I have a few papier-mache eggs from last Easter's decorations. I'll paint those pale blue and put them in the nest. The branches should protect them from the winter weather, just as they once protected those baby birds.

It's a Christmas tree, all right, and a lovely one.

When the school bus comes, the boys will shriek with delight at the sight of the tree. And Clara? I can't wait to see her face when she spots the eggs.

Table-Toppers Make Christmas The Merry Center of Attention

SANTA MAY GET most of the credit for Christmas spirit, but we know who really decks the halls, wraps the gifts, bakes the cookies, writes out the cards, plans the parties and keeps up the traditions—in addition to all her other daily chores!

So when it comes to fast and easy time-savers like these Yuletide table trims, busy holiday hostesses will want to look this way.

It doesn't take a lot of time or money to set a festive table that is sure to serve up hearty helpings of Christmas cheer—no matter what the occasion.

Fresh and Fanciful

Are friends, neighbors or unexpected guests dropping by for a last-minute caroling party or potluck supper? Not to worry. A fresh and festive centerpiece is as close as your grocery store, where you can usually pick up a bouquet of pretty red and white carnations or a small poinsettia plant.

Tuck some holly or greens around your bright blooms and set the bowl in a box wrapped to look like a gift. Red, green or white candles add a warm glow and merry finishing touch.

If no flowers are available, fill a glass bowl with chunky pinecones and bright berries from the yard, then add twists of shimmery gold and red Christmas ribbon between the cones and stems.

A Taste of Elegance

Welcome your Christmas brunch or buffet guests with an easy but elegant arrangement of luscious fresh fruits.

We set a silver tray atop a snowy doily and decked it with a pineapple, the international symbol of hospitality and friendship since Colonial days. We surrounded it with a wreath of shiny apples and cascading bunches of grapes in alternating colors of red and green. What could be more simple? You might even add a few scattered tea lights for extra sparkle.

Simply Stunning

A more sophisticated festive look can be put together in minutes with items on hand for the holidays. This simple but stunning tier (at far right) was assembled with three glass plates of different sizes separated by two small glass cups and topped with an elegant champagne glass.

The bottom layer is filled with lacy greens and shining ornaments, the second layer with loops of ribbon and baby's breath, and the top two layers with more ornaments and greens. The effect is frosty, fancy and classic Christmas!

Toys on Parade

Gather up some of the children's toys for their own special table centerpiece! We dressed our teddies in Christmas bow ties and added pretty presents (these could also hold inexpensive door prizes or take-home favors). To finish the topper, we tucked a mini tree in the middle.

But any grouping of holiday collectibles can make a jolly centerpiece for kids. Try nutcrackers, angels, snowmen, a bowl of bright ornaments, a tiny toy train or tree hung with candy canes, even "Merry Christmas" spelled out with wooden alphabet blocks.

So let your imagination go and have some fun with this year's holiday table-toppers. Because they can be fashioned in a twinkling from seasonal odds and ends you're likely to have on hand, there will be more time to enjoy your guests and all the festivities!

MAKE THE SEASON bright with these fast and festive ideas for dressing up a holiday table in minutes. With a dash of creativity, you can fashion an eye-catching centerpiece using flowers, fruits, ornaments or children's toys.

Her Homespun Figures Are 'Claus' For Celebration!

SOME PEOPLE lose sight of Santa Claus and all his magic once they grow up. But not Marilynn Ausherman.

In fact, it wasn't until retiring from her full-time job a few years ago that this great-grandmother began seeing him every day!

"I needed a project," she recalls, "so I came up with the idea of making Santa Claus dolls."

Why Santas? As a little girl, Marilynn couldn't wait for the jolly old elf to make his annual appearance. As a

grown-up, she found she still loves the notion of giving and caring that Santa represents.

From a basement workshop in the Milan, Illinois home she shares with husband Paul, a retired minister, Marilynn began making her Mill Creek Santas in 2000. "And I've been busy ever since," she says with a laugh.

Named for the winding creek behind her house, the 24-inch-tall Santa figures are a year-round labor of love.

"I keep a log of all of them," she notes, adding that it takes 8-10 hours to complete one Santa. Each is signed, numbered and truly one-of-a-kind.

Marilynn starts by using a crosscut slice of a tree as her base. St. Nick's body is crafted from PVC pipe, wooden dowels, quilt batting and wire—then secured to the wood base.

"I use a commercial head because I found one with glass eyes and a happy comforting look that appeals to children as well as adults," she explains.

Next, she adds a beard, mustache, hair and eyebrows made of wool to each head, then gets to work on the character of her figure. "The theme of each Santa develops as I create his outfit," Marilynn says.

There's the Santa bundled in green with gold rabbit fur accents, a John Deere applique across his chest and miniature tractor and wagon. Her gardener Santa is decked out in fur-trimmed denim and a straw hat, beside

SPECIAL SANTA figures echo Marilynn Ausherman's wishes for a "Merry Christmas to all"!

a tree trimmed in garden tools. And a woodsman Santa in a raccoon-trimmed suit totes snowshoes beside a bare-branched tree with bird nests and birds.

"I use only recycled fabrics and furs. I'm always looking for them at resale shops and yard sales," she adds. Accents include decorated trees and teddy bears.

"My Santas are a gift from the heart to everyone who buys one," says Marilynn, who believes "there's a little Santa in all of us as we give gifts to those we love and care about."

Editor's Note: *For more information, phone Marilynn at 1-309/787-3949 or E-mail her at pra33@msn.com.*

Photos: Chris Taylor

Dolls Are Patterned After Merry Country Holidays and Traditions

By Katie Knies of Copper Center, Alaska

A JOLLY CREW of rustic moose, bear and snow-folk dolls surrounds crafter Katie Knies. She designs and sells the patterns for all of these adorable characters through her Mountain Home Collectibles business in Alaska.

CHILDREN MAY HAVE visions of sugarplums dancing in their heads on Christmas Eve, but I have pattern designs dancing in my head all year long! They are generally geared to older "children" who enjoy detailed rustic dolls from Santas to angels, snow folk, moose and bears.

Christmas is my very favorite time of year, you see. I love my childhood memories of it, the traditions, the sense of anticipation it brings. I even listen to Christmas music all year long!

It helps put me in the mood to design the whimsical doll patterns I now sell through Mountain Home Collectibles, my small home-based business nestled in the remote community of Kenny Lake in Alaska.

Our nearest post office is 35 miles away and the nearest bank, 45 miles. But although this wilderness area gets cold in winter, you'll always find warmth among the people—just as I always find inspiration for new character dolls!

It was my mother who taught me to sew as a child. My love of sewing led me to begin stitching Santa dolls, then to market them at craft bazaars, and finally to create my own patterns so that others could share the fun and fulfillment of crafting something with their own hands.

My dolls range in size from 4 to 36 inches and most of their bodies are made from either muslin or felt. All are stuffed with polyfill, and rice is added to the bases of some sitting figures for stability. Most can be completed in 2 days, depending on painting techniques and the detail involved.

Many of my designs start with a picture or memory in my head. As I draw the design on paper, I begin making up pattern pieces. Then, sewing it up for the first time, I make notes along the way for instructions, which are very complete and thorough.

I do try to write them as if I were talking to someone. It makes it more fun for me and crafters might even feel like they're sewing with an old friend.

As for Santa? He might get a kick out of the fact that my patterns have traveled around the world nearly as far as he has—to Iceland, Holland, New Zealand, Singapore and Japan—spreading the love and spirit of this special season!

Editor's Note: *Katie's patterns can be ordered by calling her at 1-907/822-4122 or on-line at www.mountainhome collect.com.*

109

Readers Share Merry Trees

A COWBOY CHRISTMAS is the theme for Mavis LaPointe, "out West" in Hythe, Alberta.

ALL-NATURAL NOEL is Marilyn Priebe's motif for a holiday tree in her Westlake, Ohio home.

STRAW AND WHEAT weavings deck the tree of Waltraud Illias in Quakertown, Pennsylvania.

HELPING HANDS traced by grandkids trim Jeanne Porter's Poplar Bluff, Missouri tree.

GALA GRAPEVINE wears birds' nests on Virginia Buchholz's Cleveland, Wisconsin tree.

Traditions to Try

A HOLIDAY tradition can be as simple as a special food, decoration or ritual that you rely on to brighten the season! Some families share a traditional Christmas Eve meal every year, while others enjoy the same once-a-year delicacies at an annual Christmas brunch.

Oregon Baker Puts the Icing On Holiday Tradition, Season

TOO PRETTY TO EAT. Joy Denison's delicate and detailed touch with icing turns her tasty gingerbread cookies into seasonal works of art and sweet gifts from the heart.

ONCE UPON an old-world Christmas, holiday cookies and sweets were a competitive business. In Germany during the 1800s, only those bakers with proven artistry could get their hands on the white sugar needed to bake them. And in England, some bakers actually used gold leaf to trim their concoctions!

Joy Denison of Williams, Oregon could hold her own with the best of those old-time cooks.

Carrying on a tasty Yuletide tradition, her whimsically iced and trimmed gingerbread cookies have been dubbed "edible works of art". And corporations, celebrities and fans have wrapped them up as gifts, gobbled them down in delight or hung them on Christmas trees as ornaments for all to enjoy.

"Cookies should be a blessing to those who receive them," Joy says.

But her convictions weren't always that strong. "My mom got me started on cake decorating when we took a class together, but I pretty much hated it," she recalls with a smile. "Then they offered a gingerbread class, and I've been doing it ever since!

"When I first started selling my cookies in 1987, I took them to a department store and a mail-order business. Both put in orders for cookies."

Later, Joy began doing custom cookies—gingerbread pilots and mechanics for an aircraft company and little houses for various real estate firms, for instance. Her husband, Dave, created the special cutters she used.

Once owner and sole decorator of The Joy of Cookies company, Joy was filling orders for 100 cookie baskets a week from her home kitchen. "It smelled like the bakery in Santa's workshop for a quarter of a mile before you got here," she laughs.

But what does she remember most fondly about the Yuletide gingerbread Santas and sleighs, snowmen and stars, angels, nutcrackers and reindeer that garnered her so much attention?

"The treats seemed to have a special appeal for grandmothers and grandpas. I liked that. Children, too, were always wowed by them. My friend's grandson just held his nutcracker cookie and stared at it, then ran to get a pencil so he could draw it on paper and not lose the image," she remembers, laughing.

Now retired, Joy is spending more time with family, baking up sweet Christmas memories by the dozen...and teaching her grandson how to really top off this Christmas tradition.

111

I'll Never Forget...

Grandparents Played Important Part In Making Christmas Extra-Special

By Edna Bell-Pearson of Meade, Kansas

I WATCHED Grandma replace the lid and adjust the damper on the wood-burning range, then move the huge kettle of chicken and dumplings to the front of the stove. The kitchen was warm and cozy and smelled heavenly from the goodies she and Mama had prepared earlier.

It was Christmas Eve—the most exciting day of the year for this 5-year-old! And I was being allowed to help in the kitchen for the first time. I'd been assigned the task of arranging silverware on each side of the plates Grandma had placed around the big dining table.

Everything looked so festive. Candles on the buffet were lit, evergreen branches hung on the walls and a bowl of apples and oranges graced the center of the snow-white tablecloth.

We always spent Christmas with Grandma and Grandpa—it was something we looked forward to all year. While the grown-ups visited, we could play anywhere we liked in the house except the parlor—that was a no-no.

But how our excitement grew each time we spied an adult slipping through the half-closed parlor doors with a secretive smile.

Oh Christmas Tree!

When dinner was over, the parlor doors swung wide. I approached hesitantly, Grandma's hand on my back propelling me. Then I gasped, catching my breath at what was surely the most magnificent Christmas tree in the world!

A shining silver star at the top almost brushed the ceiling, and brightly wrapped packages were tucked among the branches and heaped underneath.

Best of all, perched high in the tree was a doll with golden curls and a ruffled pink dress I just knew was meant for me. It was the most beautiful doll I'd ever seen.

I was so enchanted by it all that I jumped at a sudden clatter outside and turned to see...Santa at the window!

A moment later, he actually entered the room, dressed in red, jingling his sleigh bells and shouting, "Ho, ho, ho!"

Trembling with excitement, I managed to say "thank you" for my bag of candy before Santa patted me on the head, gave his sleigh bells a mighty shake and danced out the door, leaving a roomful of children speechless.

Minutes later, Grandpa, who'd gone to check the livestock, returned and we crowded around to tell him how he had just missed seeing Santa Claus!

"But I did see him," Grandpa insisted, as excited as we were. "He was just getting into his sleigh as I came out of the barn...why, he even waved to me! Come along now and let's see what he left under the tree."

Magical Memories

I remember that Christmas as the very happiest of my whole life.

A few months later, I was sent to stay with my grandparents for a while. That was fine with me because I liked nothing better than spending time with them.

One spring evening, I was helping Grandma feed the chickens. "You get the feed while I gather the eggs," she said.

In the feed shed, gunnysacks of cracked corn and bran vied for floor space with garden tools and storage boxes. Saddles, bridles and harnesses crowded the walls.

Picking up the feed pan, I was reaching for a scoop on a nearby shelf when I brushed against something hanging on the wall and heard a familiar jingle.

For a moment, my heart stopped.

I stared at the object, transfixed. It looked—and sounded—exactly like those bells of Santa's. What could it mean? And then I knew!

"Grandma," I shouted, running to the henhouse, the feed totally forgotten. "Grandma, I know who Santa Claus is!"

How often I have wished I could experience again the warmth and utter joy I felt that Christmas. Perhaps that's why I so treasured the doll with the golden curls well into my adult years. It was a fond memory of my happiest and most exciting Christmas ever!

May you share the shining peace and promise of this holiday season with your family and friends throughout the coming year.

INDEX

Share Your Holiday Joy!

DO *YOU* celebrate Christmas in a special way? If so, we'd like to know! We're already gathering material for our next *Country Woman Christmas* book. And we need your help!

Do you have a nostalgic holiday-related story to share? Perhaps you have penned a Christmas poem…or a heartwarming fiction story?

Does your family carry on a favorite holiday tradition? Or do you deck your halls in some festive way? Maybe you know of a Christmas-loving country woman others might like to meet?

We're looking for *original* Christmas quilt patterns and craft projects, plus homemade Nativities, gingerbread houses, etc. Don't forget to include your best recipes for holiday-favorite main-dish meats, home-baked cookies, candies, breads, etc.!

Send your ideas and photos to "*CW* Christmas Book", 5925 Country Lane, Greendale WI 53129. (Enclose a self-addressed stamped envelope if you'd like materials returned.)